Grade **5**

This Book Belongs To:

Math on Target

Using Thinking Maps to Solve
Multiple-Choice, Short-Answer, and
Extended-Response Problems

Written By:
Yolande F. Grizinski, Ed.D.
Leslie Holzhauser-Peters, MS. CCC-SP
Claire L. Crook, Ph.D.

Show What You Know® Publishing

Published By:

Show What You Know® Publishing
A Division of Englefield & Associates, Inc.
P.O. Box 341348
Columbus, OH 43234-1348
614-764-1211

www.showwhatyouknowpublishing.com

Printed in the United States of America
07 06 05   20 19 18 17 16 15 14 13 12 11 10 9 8 7 6 5 4 3 2 1

ISBN: 1-59230-111-8

About the Authors

Yolande F. Grizinski received a Bachelor's degree from Miami University, a Master's degree from Wright State University, and a Doctorate in Education from the University of Cincinnati. She has worked in public education for 30 years as a curriculum consultant in the areas of language arts with a focus on writing assessment. She is currently the Assistant Superintendent of the Warren County Educational Service Center in Lebanon, Ohio.

Leslie Holzhauser-Peters holds a Bachelor's degree from the University of Cincinnati and a Master's degree from Miami University. She has 27 years of experience working in public schools in Special Education as a Speech-language pathologist, as a Supervisor, and currently as a Curriculum Consultant. Her areas of expertise are language, literacy, and intervention.

Claire L. Crook holds a Bachelor's degree from The Ohio State University, a Master's degree from Xavier University, and a Doctorate in Mathematics Education from The Ohio State University. She has more than 30 years experience in public education as teacher, administrator, and consultant. She is currently a Mathematics Curriculum Consultant.

The authors met at the Warren County Educational Service Center in Lebanon, Ohio. There they developed and implemented a host of language arts and mathematics initiatives.

Acknowledgements

Show What You Know® Publishing acknowledges the following for their efforts in making this assessment preparation material available for students, parents, and teachers.

Cindi Englefield, President/Publisher
Eloise Boehm-Sasala, Vice President/Managing Editor
Lainie Burke, Project Editor/Graphic Designer
Erin Richers, Project Editor
Rob Ciccotelli, Project Editor
Christine Filippetti, Project Editor
Jill Borish, Project Editor
Jennifer Harney, Illustrator/Cover Designer

Content Reviewer:
Kathie Christian

© 2005 Englefield & Associates, Inc.

Table of Contents

Introduction vii

Chapter 1: Number Sense 1
   Model Problem 1: Multiple-Choice 2
   Practice Problems 1–7 5
   Model Problem 2: Short-Answer 19
   Practice Problems 8–9 22
   Model Problem 3: Extended-Response 26
   Practice Problem 10 29

Chapter 2: Measurement 31
   Model Problem 4: Multiple-Choice 32
   Practice Problems 11–17 35
   Model Problem 5: Short-Answer 49
   Practice Problems 18–19 52
   Model Problem 6: Extended-Response 56
   Practice Problem 20 59

Chapter 3: Geometry 61
   Model Problem 7: Multiple-Choice 62
   Practice Problems 21–27 65
   Model Problem 8: Short-Answer 79
   Practice Problems 28–29 82
   Model Problem 9: Extended-Response 86
   Practice Problem 30 89

Chapter 4: Algebra 91
   Model Problem 10: Multiple-Choice 92
   Practice Problems 31–37 95
   Model Problem 11: Short-Answer 109
   Practice Problems 38–39 112
   Model Problem 12: Extended-Response 116
   Practice Problem 40 119

Table of Contents

Chapter 5: Data and Probability **121**

Model Problem 13: Multiple-Choice 122

Practice Problems 41–47 125

Model Problem 14: Short-Answer 139

Practice Problems 48–49 142

Model Problem 15: Extended-Response 146

Practice Problem 50 149

Chapter 6: Manipulatives **153**

Introduction

The Purpose of Math on Target

By the time you reach fifth grade, you are expected to analyze and solve multi-step problems. You are expected to explain the strategies you use and to describe change. Your goal should be to apply the mathematics you learn in school to everyday, real-world situations. *Math on Target* was developed for the following purposes:

1. To provide you with a step-by-step way to look at word problems. By using the thinking maps provided, you will be able to explain your problem-solving strategies.

2. To provide you with three types of problems—multiple-choice, short-answer, and extended-response. These types of problems involve
   - Number Sense
   - Measurement
   - Geometry
   - Algebra
   - Data and Probability

We hope *Math on Target*'s thinking map will help you solve mathematics problems today and in your future.

Chapter 1

Number Sense

What is Number Sense?

Number Sense involves your ability to understand numbers by representing them and recognizing the relationships among different number systems.

You are learning to use

- Fractions
- Decimals
- Percents
- Numbers less than zero

You will also continue to solve problems that involve multiplication and division. Finally, you will solve problems using the rules for order of operations.

What does Number Sense look like?

- You will use pictures, graphs, grids, and other tools to represent fractions and percents.
- You will discover how to write the same number as a decimal, a fraction, or a percent.
- You will be able to explain the order of operations.
  1. Parentheses
  2. Exponents
  3. Multiplication
  4. Division
  5. Addition
  6. Subtraction
- You will determine the common denominator.
- You will add and subtract fractions.
- You will use mental math to estimate answers.
- You will determine whether your answer makes sense.

DO NOT COPY

Model Problem 1:
Number Sense
Multiple-Choice

1. Three fifth-grade classes have the same number of students. When one teacher is absent, the students from that teacher's class are equally divided between the other two classes. In this situation, 13 students will be placed in each classroom. How many fifth-grade students are there in all three classes?

   ○ A. 26

   ○ B. 39

   ○ C. 78

   ○ D. 52

Use the thinking map on the next page to solve the problem.
Fill in the circle next to the correct answer.
Mark only one answer.

DO NOT COPY

4

Thinking Map

Read the Problem	☐ Read the Problem
Reread the Problem	☐ Reread the Problem
Write the important math vocabulary that tells you what to do.	
Reread the Problem	☐ Reread the Problem
What information do you have that you can use to solve the problem? Can you get clues from: ☐ The answer choices ☐ Pictures, charts, or graphs ☐ A problem you have solved before	
Reread the Problem	☐ Reread the Problem
Solve the problem. Use one or more: ☐ Act it out. ☐ Use manipulatives. You can: ☐ Do a calculation: addition, subtraction, multiplication, or division. ☐ Draw a picture, graph, or table. ☐ Set up an equation. ☐ Write a formula.	
Use words, pictures, or numbers to explain your answer.	
Does your answer make sense? Why or why not?	
Answer the Problem	☐ Be sure to give your answer on the previous page

One Way to Complete the Thinking Map

Read the Problem	☑ Read the Problem
Reread the Problem	☑ Reread the Problem
Write the important math vocabulary that tells you what to do.	equally divide how many in all
Reread the Problem	☑ Reread the Problem
What information do you have that you can use to solve the problem? Can you get clues from: ☑ The answer choices ☐ Pictures, charts, or graphs ☑ A problem you have solved before	3 classes same number of students per class one class divided into 2 groups of 13
Reread the Problem	☑ Reread the Problem
Solve the problem. Use one or more: ☐ Act it out. ☐ Use manipulatives. You can: ☐ Do a calculation: addition, subtraction, multiplication, or division. ☑ Draw a picture, graph, or table. ☑ Set up an equation. ☐ Write a formula.	$\boxed{\textbf{Class A}}$ $\boxed{\textbf{Class B}}$ $\boxed{\textbf{Class C}}$ +13 +13 ÷ into 2 groups 13 + 13 = Class C A = B = C 13 + 13 = 26 26 = 26 = 26 26 × 3 = 78
Use words, pictures, or numbers to explain your answer.	Setting up an equation: Total: A = B = C A + B + C C = 13 + 13 26 + 26 + 26 = 78 A = 13 + 13 B = 13 + 13 C is the correct answer.
Does your answer make sense? Why or why not?	Yes—26 students is a reasonable number for a class size.
Answer the Problem	☑ Be sure to give your answer on the previous page

     © 2005 Englefield & Associates, Inc.

Number Sense
Multiple-Choice Practice Problem 1

1. The fabric store has one-yard fabric remnants on sale for $0.99. Neela needs to buy $\frac{1}{2}$ yard and $\frac{3}{8}$ yard of fabric. What is the least number of remnants she needs to buy?

    ○ A. 1
    ○ B. 2
    ○ C. 3
    ○ D. 4

**Use the thinking map on the next page to solve the problem.
Fill in the circle next to the correct answer.
Mark only one answer.**

Thinking Map

Read the Problem	☐ Read the Problem
Reread the Problem	☐ Reread the Problem
Write the important math vocabulary that tells you what to do.	
Reread the Problem	☐ Reread the Problem
What information do you have that you can use to solve the problem? Can you get clues from: ☐ The answer choices ☐ Pictures, charts, or graphs ☐ A problem you have solved before	
Reread the Problem	☐ Reread the Problem
Solve the problem. Use one or more: ☐ Act it out. ☐ Use manipulatives. You can: ☐ Do a calculation: addition, subtraction, multiplication, or division. ☐ Draw a picture, graph, or table. ☐ Set up an equation. ☐ Write a formula.	
Use words, pictures, or numbers to explain your answer.	
Does your answer make sense? Why or why not?	
Answer the Problem	☐ Be sure to give your answer on the previous page

Number Sense
Multiple-Choice Practice Problem 2

2. Rainfall was recorded in the morning and in the afternoon for four days in April. On which day was the total rainfall between $\frac{1}{2}$ inch and 1 inch?

April 3: $\frac{4}{8}$ inch and $\frac{1}{3}$ inch

April 10: $\frac{1}{16}$ inch and $\frac{5}{16}$ inch

April 15: $\frac{3}{5}$ inch and $\frac{4}{5}$ inch

April 22: 1 inch and $\frac{1}{2}$ inch

○ A. April 3

○ B. April 10

○ C. April 15

○ D. April 22

Use the thinking map on the next page to solve the problem.
Fill in the circle next to the correct answer.
Mark only one answer.

DO NOT COPY

Thinking Map

Read the Problem	☐ Read the Problem
Reread the Problem	☐ Reread the Problem
Write the important math vocabulary that tells you what to do.	
Reread the Problem	☐ Reread the Problem
What information do you have that you can use to solve the problem? Can you get clues from: ☐ The answer choices ☐ Pictures, charts, or graphs ☐ A problem you have solved before	
Reread the Problem	☐ Reread the Problem
Solve the problem. Use one or more: ☐ Act it out. ☐ Use manipulatives. You can: ☐ Do a calculation: addition, subtraction, multiplication, or division. ☐ Draw a picture, graph, or table. ☐ Set up an equation. ☐ Write a formula.	
Use words, pictures, or numbers to explain your answer.	
Does your answer make sense? Why or why not?	
Answer the Problem	☐ Be sure to give your answer on the previous page

Number Sense
Multiple-Choice Practice Problem 3

3. The following problem was given to the class. Students used different approaches to solve the problem. The equations below show how **each student started to solve the problem**. Which approach would most likely lead to a WRONG answer?

Problem: 16 x 31

- ○ A. 16 x 10 = 160
- ○ B. 4 x 31 = 124
- ○ C. (10 x 30) + (6 x 1) = 16 x 31
- ○ D. (16 x 30) + 16

Use the thinking map on the next page to solve the problem.
Fill in the circle next to the correct answer.
Mark only one answer.

Thinking Map

Read the Problem	☐ Read the Problem
Reread the Problem	☐ Reread the Problem
Write the important math vocabulary that tells you what to do.	
Reread the Problem	☐ Reread the Problem
What information do you have that you can use to solve the problem? Can you get clues from: ☐ The answer choices ☐ Pictures, charts, or graphs ☐ A problem you have solved before	
Reread the Problem	☐ Reread the Problem
Solve the problem. Use one or more: ☐ Act it out. ☐ Use manipulatives. You can: ☐ Do a calculation: addition, subtraction, multiplication, or division. ☐ Draw a picture, graph, or table. ☐ Set up an equation. ☐ Write a formula.	
Use words, pictures, or numbers to explain your answer.	
Does your answer make sense? Why or why not?	
Answer the Problem	☐ Be sure to give your answer on the previous page

DO NOT COPY

Number Sense
Multiple-Choice Practice Problem 4

4. Kathy had $30. Jim had no money, so he borrowed $20 from Kathy. Kathy borrowed $10 from Jim. Then, Jim borrowed $20 from Kathy. From the information given, which statement is true?

○ A. More information is needed to find who has more money.

○ B. Kathy has more money than Jim.

○ C. Jim and Kathy have the same amount of money.

○ D. Jim has more money than Kathy.

**Use the thinking map on the next page to solve the problem.
Fill in the circle next to the correct answer.
Mark only one answer.**

Thinking Map

Read the Problem	☐ Read the Problem
Reread the Problem	☐ Reread the Problem
Write the important math vocabulary that tells you what to do.	
Reread the Problem	☐ Reread the Problem
What information do you have that you can use to solve the problem? Can you get clues from: ☐ The answer choices ☐ Pictures, charts, or graphs ☐ A problem you have solved before	
Reread the Problem	☐ Reread the Problem
Solve the problem. Use one or more: ☐ Act it out. ☐ Use manipulatives. You can: ☐ Do a calculation: addition, subtraction, multiplication, or division. ☐ Draw a picture, graph, or table. ☐ Set up an equation. ☐ Write a formula.	
Use words, pictures, or numbers to explain your answer.	
Does your answer make sense? Why or why not?	
Answer the Problem	☐ Be sure to give your answer on the previous page

Number Sense
Multiple-Choice Practice Problem 5

5. The grid below is a diagram of a tiled classroom floor. The custodian cleaned the shaded portion of the floor before he ran out of cleaning solution. Which percent represents the uncleaned portion of the floor, and which fraction represents the cleaned portion of the floor?

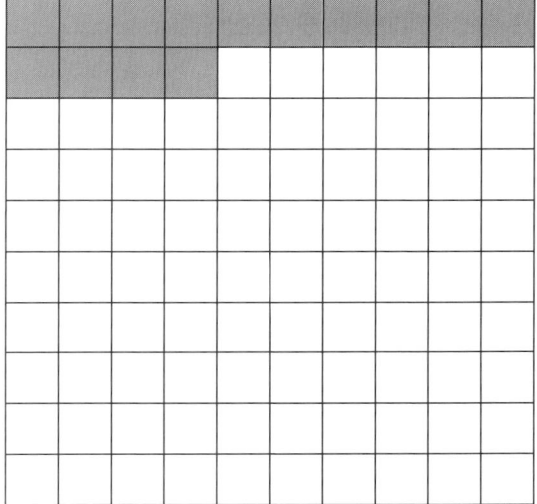

○ A. 86% and $\dfrac{24}{100}$

○ B. 86% and $\dfrac{7}{50}$

○ C. 80% and $\dfrac{1}{5}$

○ D. 85% and $\dfrac{85}{100}$

Use the thinking map on the next page to solve the problem.
Fill in the circle next to the correct answer.
Mark only one answer.

Thinking Map

Read the Problem	☐ Read the Problem
Reread the Problem	☐ Reread the Problem
Write the important math vocabulary that tells you what to do.	
Reread the Problem	☐ Reread the Problem
What information do you have that you can use to solve the problem? Can you get clues from: ☐ The answer choices ☐ Pictures, charts, or graphs ☐ A problem you have solved before	
Reread the Problem	☐ Reread the Problem
Solve the problem. Use one or more: ☐ Act it out. ☐ Use manipulatives. You can: ☐ Do a calculation: addition, subtraction, multiplication, or division. ☐ Draw a picture, graph, or table. ☐ Set up an equation. ☐ Write a formula.	
Use words, pictures, or numbers to explain your answer.	
Does your answer make sense? Why or why not?	
Answer the Problem	☐ Be sure to give your answer on the previous page

Number Sense
Multiple-Choice Practice Problem 6

6. Jay missed 3 out of 4 problems on a math test. The problems, along with Jay's answers, are shown below. Which problem did Jay get correct?

   ○ A. $0.3 + 0.24 = 0.27$

   ○ B. $0.3 + 0.24 = 0.54$

   ○ C. $.03 + .02 + 0.4 = .9$

   ○ D. $3.0 + 2.4 = .54$

Use the thinking map on the next page to solve the problem.
Fill in the circle next to the correct answer.
Mark only one answer.

Thinking Map

Read the Problem	☐ Read the Problem
Reread the Problem	☐ Reread the Problem
Write the important math vocabulary that tells you what to do.	
Reread the Problem	☐ Reread the Problem
What information do you have that you can use to solve the problem? Can you get clues from: ☐ The answer choices ☐ Pictures, charts, or graphs ☐ A problem you have solved before	
Reread the Problem	☐ Reread the Problem
Solve the problem. Use one or more: ☐ Act it out. ☐ Use manipulatives. You can: ☐ Do a calculation: addition, subtraction, multiplication, or division. ☐ Draw a picture, graph, or table. ☐ Set up an equation. ☐ Write a formula.	
Use words, pictures, or numbers to explain your answer.	
Does your answer make sense? Why or why not?	
Answer the Problem	☐ Be sure to give your answer on the previous page

Number Sense
Multiple-Choice Practice Problem 7

7. Ben's mathematics grade average was 88.8% the first week of school. His grades for the first four days are shown on the chart below.

Monday	98%
Tuesday	96%
Wednesday	88%
Thursday	89%

What was his mathematics grade on Friday?

- A. 95%
- B. 87.8%
- C. 83%
- D. 73%

**Use the thinking map on the next page to solve the problem.
Fill in the circle next to the correct answer.
Mark only one answer.**

Thinking Map

Read the Problem	☐ Read the Problem
Reread the Problem	☐ Reread the Problem
Write the important math vocabulary that tells you what to do.	
Reread the Problem	☐ Reread the Problem
What information do you have that you can use to solve the problem? Can you get clues from: ☐ The answer choices ☐ Pictures, charts, or graphs ☐ A problem you have solved before	
Reread the Problem	☐ Reread the Problem
Solve the problem. Use one or more: ☐ Act it out. ☐ Use manipulatives. You can: ☐ Do a calculation: addition, subtraction, multiplication, or division. ☐ Draw a picture, graph, or table. ☐ Set up an equation. ☐ Write a formula.	
Use words, pictures, or numbers to explain your answer.	
Does your answer make sense? Why or why not?	
Answer the Problem	☐ Be sure to give your answer on the previous page

DO NOT COPY

Model Problem 2:
Number Sense
Short-Answer

2. A pet store owner wants to make gift packages for customers who purchase puppies. He has 42 tennis balls, 73 rawhide chews, and 36 squeaky toys. What is the greatest number of identical bags he can make? What will be contained in each bag?

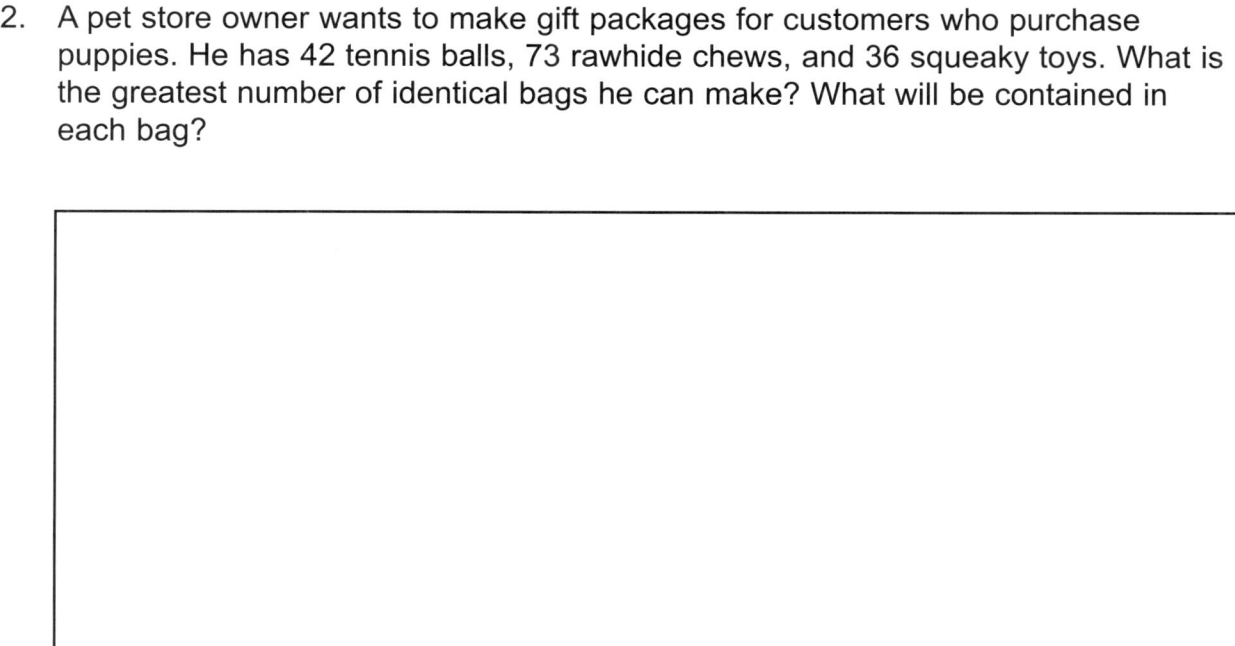

Use the thinking map on the next page to solve the problem.
Write your answer in the box.

Thinking Map

Read the Problem	☐ Read the Problem
Reread the Problem	☐ Reread the Problem
Write the important math vocabulary that tells you what to do.	
Reread the Problem	☐ Reread the Problem
What information do you have that you can use to solve the problem? Can you get clues from: ☐ The answer choices ☐ Pictures, charts, or graphs ☐ A problem you have solved before	
Reread the Problem	☐ Reread the Problem
Solve the problem. Use one or more: ☐ Act it out. ☐ Use manipulatives. You can: ☐ Do a calculation: addition, subtraction, multiplication, or division. ☐ Draw a picture, graph, or table. ☐ Set up an equation. ☐ Write a formula.	
Use words, pictures, or numbers to explain your answer.	
Does your answer make sense? Why or why not?	
Answer the Problem	☐ Be sure to give your answer on the previous page

  © 2005 Englefield & Associates, Inc.

One Way to Complete the Thinking Map

Read the Problem	✓ Read the Problem
Reread the Problem	✓ Reread the Problem
Write the important math vocabulary that tells you what to do.	How many identical greatest number
Reread the Problem	✓ Reread the Problem
What information do you have that you can use to solve the problem? Can you get clues from: ☐ The answer choices ☐ Pictures, charts, or graphs ✓ A problem you have solved before	42 tennis balls 73 rawhide chews 36 squeaky toys
Reread the Problem	✓ Reread the Problem
Solve the problem. Use one or more: ☐ Act it out. ✓ Use manipulatives. You can: ✓ Do a calculation: addition, subtraction, multiplication, or division. ✓ Draw a picture, graph, or table. ✓ Set up an equation. ☐ Write a formula.	Since 36 items is the smallest number of items, 36 is the greatest number of bags he can make. To find the greatest number of items per bag, subtract 36 from the number of each item to find out how many will be used for each bag (or divide the number of each item by 36). Squeaky toy: 36 − 36 = 0; 1 per bag Rawhide chew: 73 − 36 − 36 = 1; 2 per bag Tennis ball: 42 − 36 = 6; 1 per bag
Use words, pictures, or numbers to explain your answer.	The key word is identical. If all bags are the same, you can only make as many as the smallest number of items you have. The least number is 36 (squeaky toys). Since 73 is 36 x 2 + 1, you can use two chew toys in each bag. 42 − 36 = 6; you have enough to use 1 tennis ball in each bag.
Does your answer make sense? Why or why not?	Yes: each bag contains 1 squeaky toy, 2 rawhide chews, and 1 tennis ball.
Answer the Problem	✓ Be sure to give your answer on the previous page

Number Sense
Short-Answer Practice Problem 8

8. Margie brought $3\frac{1}{4}$ pounds of candy to the Halloween party at school. Jeff brought 5.5 pounds, and Karla brought $4\frac{3}{4}$ pounds. How many pounds do they have altogether? Your answer may be written in mixed number or decimal format.

**Use the thinking map on the next page to solve the problem.
Write your answer in the box.**

DO NOT COPY

Thinking Map

Read the Problem	☐ Read the Problem
Reread the Problem	☐ Reread the Problem
Write the important math vocabulary that tells you what to do.	
Reread the Problem	☐ Reread the Problem
What information do you have that you can use to solve the problem? Can you get clues from: ☐ The answer choices ☐ Pictures, charts, or graphs ☐ A problem you have solved before	
Reread the Problem	☐ Reread the Problem
Solve the problem. Use one or more: ☐ Act it out. ☐ Use manipulatives. You can: ☐ Do a calculation: addition, subtraction, multiplication, or division. ☐ Draw a picture, graph, or table. ☐ Set up an equation. ☐ Write a formula.	
Use words, pictures, or numbers to explain your answer.	
Does your answer make sense? Why or why not?	
Answer the Problem	☐ Be sure to give your answer on the previous page

Number Sense
Short-Answer Practice Problem 9

9. Estimate which fraction is the smallest and which is the largest. Order these fractions from smallest to largest in your head. Explain your reasoning.

$$\frac{3}{5}, \frac{7}{10}, \frac{1}{2}, \frac{3}{4}$$

Use the thinking map on the next page to solve the problem.
Write your answer in the box.

DO NOT COPY

Thinking Map

Read the Problem	☐ Read the Problem
Reread the Problem	☐ Reread the Problem
Write the important math vocabulary that tells you what to do.	
Reread the Problem	☐ Reread the Problem
What information do you have that you can use to solve the problem? Can you get clues from: ☐ The answer choices ☐ Pictures, charts, or graphs ☐ A problem you have solved before	
Reread the Problem	☐ Reread the Problem
Solve the problem. Use one or more: ☐ Act it out. ☐ Use manipulatives. You can: ☐ Do a calculation: addition, subtraction, multiplication, or division. ☐ Draw a picture, graph, or table. ☐ Set up an equation. ☐ Write a formula.	
Use words, pictures, or numbers to explain your answer.	
Does your answer make sense? Why or why not?	
Answer the Problem	☐ Be sure to give your answer on the previous page

Model Problem 3:
Number Sense
Extended-Response

3. Carlos applied for two different jobs. One pays $440 per week for a 35-hour work week. The other pays $11.50 per hour for a 40-hour work week. Which job pays more per hour? If you were Carlos, which job would you take? Explain your answer.

**Use the thinking map on the next page to solve the problem.
Write your answer in the box.**

 © 2005 Englefield & Associates, Inc.

Thinking Map

Read the Problem	☐ Read the Problem
Reread the Problem	☐ Reread the Problem
Write the important math vocabulary that tells you what to do.	
Reread the Problem	☐ Reread the Problem
What information do you have that you can use to solve the problem? Can you get clues from: ☐ The answer choices ☐ Pictures, charts, or graphs ☐ A problem you have solved before	
Reread the Problem	☐ Reread the Problem
Solve the problem. Use one or more: ☐ Act it out. ☐ Use manipulatives. You can: ☐ Do a calculation: addition, subtraction, multiplication, or division. ☐ Draw a picture, graph, or table. ☐ Set up an equation. ☐ Write a formula.	
Use words, pictures, or numbers to explain your answer.	
Does your answer make sense? Why or why not?	
Answer the Problem	☐ Be sure to give your answer on the previous page

One Way to Complete the Thinking Map

Read the Problem	☑ Read the Problem
Reread the Problem	☑ Reread the Problem
Write the important math vocabulary that tells you what to do.	per week 35-hour week per hour 40-hour week
Reread the Problem	☑ Reread the Problem
What information do you have that you can use to solve the problem? Can you get clues from: ☐ The answer choices ☐ Pictures, charts, or graphs ☑ A problem you have solved before	$440 per 35-hour week compared to $11.50 per hour for 40-hour week
Reread the Problem	☑ Reread the Problem
Solve the problem. Use one or more: ☑ Act it out. ☐ Use manipulatives. You can: ☑ Do a calculation: addition, subtraction, multiplication, or division. ☑ Draw a picture, graph, or table. ☑ Set up an equation. ☐ Write a formula.	Job 2 pays more per week. Job 1 pays less, but you work 5 hours less. Job 1 pays more per hour. To compare jobs on equal basis, calculate and compare salary per hour for both jobs. $440 ÷ 35 = $12.57 per hour; compare to $11.50 per hour.

Use words, pictures, or numbers to explain your answer.	Compare both salaries per week: Job 1: $440 per week for 35 hours Job 2: $11.50 x 40 = $460 per week	

	Job 1	Job 2	
	35	40	hours/week
	$440	$460	salary/week
	$12.57	$11.50	salary/hour

Does your answer make sense? Why or why not?	Yes. To make a comparison, you must compare like components.
Answer the Problem	☑ Be sure to give your answer on the previous page

 © 2005 Englefield & Associates, Inc.

Number Sense
Extended-Response Practice Problem 10

10. Six families live on Commons Court. One house is empty. Use the clues below to figure out where each family lives.

   A. The Joneses live between the Changs and the Browns.

   B. The Balcoms live on the cul-de-sac.

   C. The Changs live Northeast of the Balcoms.

   D. The empty house is between the Posts and the Greens.

   E. The Greens live across from the Browns.

Use the thinking map on the next page to solve the problem.
Write your answer in the box.

Thinking Map

Read the Problem	☐ Read the Problem
Reread the Problem	☐ Reread the Problem
Write the important math vocabulary that tells you what to do.	
Reread the Problem	☐ Reread the Problem
What information do you have that you can use to solve the problem? Can you get clues from: ☐ The answer choices ☐ Pictures, charts, or graphs ☐ A problem you have solved before	
Reread the Problem	☐ Reread the Problem
Solve the problem. Use one or more: ☐ Act it out. ☐ Use manipulatives. You can: ☐ Do a calculation: addition, subtraction, multiplication, or division. ☐ Draw a picture, graph, or table. ☐ Set up an equation. ☐ Write a formula.	
Use words, pictures, or numbers to explain your answer.	
Does your answer make sense? Why or why not?	
Answer the Problem	☐ Be sure to give your answer on the previous page

Chapter 2

Measurement

What is Measurement?

You are learning

- To measure and draw angles

- How and when to convert U.S. customary units and metric measurement systems (e.g., change centimeters to meters)

- To use formulas to find the perimeter and area of triangles, rectangles, and parallelograms

- How to measure surface area and volume of real objects

What does Measurement look like?

- You will know about different types of angles and how to measure them.

- You will know how to make measurements and convert (change) them to make things easier to measure.

- You will learn formulas to use as you measure the perimeters and areas of your school and classroom.

- You will use real objects and learn to measure their area and volume.

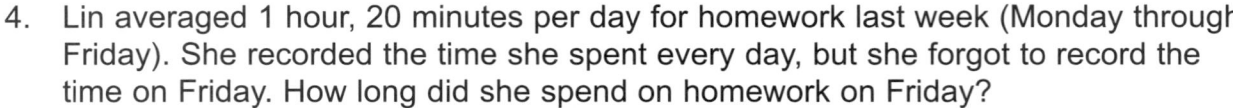

Model Problem 4:
Measurement
Multiple-Choice

4. Lin averaged 1 hour, 20 minutes per day for homework last week (Monday through Friday). She recorded the time she spent every day, but she forgot to record the time on Friday. How long did she spend on homework on Friday?

Monday	1 hour, 30 min.
Tuesday	2 hours, 10 min.
Wednesday	55 minutes
Thursday	1 hour, 25 min.

○ A. 90 minutes

○ B. 40 minutes

○ C. 1 hour, 45 minutes

○ D. 1 hour, 10 minutes

**Use the thinking map on the next page to solve the problem.
Fill in the circle next to the correct answer.
Mark only one answer.**

DO NOT COPY

Thinking Map

Read the Problem	☐ Read the Problem
Reread the Problem	☐ Reread the Problem
Write the important math vocabulary that tells you what to do.	
Reread the Problem	☐ Reread the Problem
What information do you have that you can use to solve the problem? Can you get clues from: ☐ The answer choices ☐ Pictures, charts, or graphs ☐ A problem you have solved before	
Reread the Problem	☐ Reread the Problem
Solve the problem. Use one or more: ☐ Act it out. ☐ Use manipulatives. You can: ☐ Do a calculation: addition, subtraction, multiplication, or division. ☐ Draw a picture, graph, or table. ☐ Set up an equation. ☐ Write a formula.	
Use words, pictures, or numbers to explain your answer.	
Does your answer make sense? Why or why not?	
Answer the Problem	☐ Be sure to give your answer on the previous page

One Way to Complete the Thinking Map

Read the Problem	☑ Read the Problem
Reread the Problem	☑ Reread the Problem
Write the important math vocabulary that tells you what to do.	average minutes hours
Reread the Problem	☑ Reread the Problem

What information do you have that you can use to solve the problem? Can you get clues from: ☑ The answer choices ☑ Pictures, charts, or graphs ☑ A problem you have solved before	Monday	1 hour, 30 min.
	Tuesday	2 hours, 10 min.
	Wednesday	55 minutes
	Thursday	1 hour, 25 min.

Reread the Problem	☑ Reread the Problem

Solve the problem. Use one or more: ☐ Act it out. ☐ Use manipulatives. You can: ☑ Do a calculation: addition, subtraction, multiplication, or division. ☐ Draw a picture, graph, or table. ☐ Set up an equation. ☐ Write a formula.	Add Monday–Thursday homework: 1 hour 30 min. 2 hour 10 min. 55 min. 1 hour 25 min. 4 hour 120 min. 120 minutes = 2 hours 4 hours + 2 hours = 6 hours total She spent 40 minutes studying on Friday.	1 hour 20 minutes x 5 5 hours 100 minutes 6 hours 40 minutes (total in one week) – 6 hours (total 4 days) = 40 minutes on Friday

Use words, pictures, or numbers to explain your answer.	Write an equation: $x \div 5 = 1$ hr. 20 min. $x = 6$ hr. 40 min.; x = total # of hours studying all week 6 hrs. = total # of hours spent Mon.–Thurs. 6 hrs. 40 min. – 6 hrs. = total studied on Friday
Does your answer make sense? Why or why not?	Yes—40 minutes was the time spent studying on Friday. 40 min. is in the reasonable range for an answer.
Answer the Problem	☑ Be sure to give your answer on the previous page

Measurement
Multiple-Choice Practice Problem 11

11. Miguel offered to help his Aunt Selena, a teacher, grade papers. Aunt Selena said Miguel could help her if he could tell which student had made an error in a set of papers. Miguel said that all of the equations were correct. Three of the equations are listed below. Do you agree with Miguel? If not, mark the incorrect equation.

  ○ A. 7 yards 2 feet = $7\frac{2}{3}$ yards = $6\frac{5}{3}$ yards = 7.66 yards

  ○ B. 3 lb 8 oz = $3\frac{1}{2}$ lb = $2\frac{3}{2}$ lb = 3.5 lb

  ○ C. 5 gallons 1 quart = $5\frac{1}{4}$ gallons = $4\frac{3}{4}$ gallons = 5.25 gallons

  ○ D. I agree with Miguel; all the equations are correct.

**Use the thinking map on the next page to solve the problem.
Fill in the circle next to the correct answer.
Mark only one answer.**

Thinking Map

Read the Problem	☐ Read the Problem
Reread the Problem	☐ Reread the Problem
Write the important math vocabulary that tells you what to do.	
Reread the Problem	☐ Reread the Problem
What information do you have that you can use to solve the problem? Can you get clues from: ☐ The answer choices ☐ Pictures, charts, or graphs ☐ A problem you have solved before	
Reread the Problem	☐ Reread the Problem
Solve the problem. Use one or more: ☐ Act it out. ☐ Use manipulatives. You can: ☐ Do a calculation: addition, subtraction, multiplication, or division. ☐ Draw a picture, graph, or table. ☐ Set up an equation. ☐ Write a formula.	
Use words, pictures, or numbers to explain your answer.	
Does your answer make sense? Why or why not?	
Answer the Problem	☐ Be sure to give your answer on the previous page

Measurement
Multiple-Choice Practice Problem 12

12. The school policy states that the temperature must be at least 20 degrees Fahrenheit for students to be allowed outside for recess. On Wednesday, the temperature in the morning before school was -10° F. By 9:30 a.m., it rose 13 degrees, and by 11:30 a.m., it rose 12 degrees more. What was the temperature outside at 11:30 a.m.?

○ A. 35° F

○ B. 15° F

○ C. 25° F

○ D. 20° F

Use the thinking map on the next page to solve the problem.
Fill in the circle next to the correct answer.
Mark only one answer.

Thinking Map

Read the Problem	☐ Read the Problem
Reread the Problem	☐ Reread the Problem
Write the important math vocabulary that tells you what to do.	
Reread the Problem	☐ Reread the Problem
What information do you have that you can use to solve the problem? Can you get clues from: ☐ The answer choices ☐ Pictures, charts, or graphs ☐ A problem you have solved before	
Reread the Problem	☐ Reread the Problem
Solve the problem. Use one or more: ☐ Act it out. ☐ Use manipulatives. You can: ☐ Do a calculation: addition, subtraction, multiplication, or division. ☐ Draw a picture, graph, or table. ☐ Set up an equation. ☐ Write a formula.	
Use words, pictures, or numbers to explain your answer.	
Does your answer make sense? Why or why not?	
Answer the Problem	☐ Be sure to give your answer on the previous page

 © 2005 Englefield & Associates, Inc.

Measurement
Multiple-Choice Practice Problem 13

13. What is the measure of angle D?

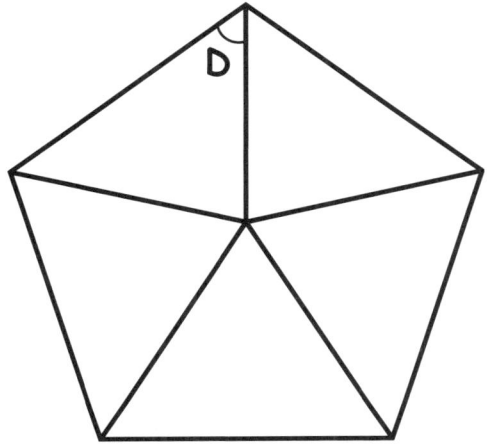

○ A. $180° \div 3$

○ B. $\dfrac{360° \div 6}{2}$

○ C. $360° \div 12$

○ D. $\dfrac{180° - 72°}{2}$

Use the thinking map on the next page to solve the problem.
Fill in the circle next to the correct answer.
Mark only one answer.

Thinking Map

Read the Problem	☐ Read the Problem
Reread the Problem	☐ Reread the Problem
Write the important math vocabulary that tells you what to do.	
Reread the Problem	☐ Reread the Problem
What information do you have that you can use to solve the problem? Can you get clues from: ☐ The answer choices ☐ Pictures, charts, or graphs ☐ A problem you have solved before	
Reread the Problem	☐ Reread the Problem
Solve the problem. Use one or more: ☐ Act it out. ☐ Use manipulatives. You can: ☐ Do a calculation: addition, subtraction, multiplication, or division. ☐ Draw a picture, graph, or table. ☐ Set up an equation. ☐ Write a formula.	
Use words, pictures, or numbers to explain your answer.	
Does your answer make sense? Why or why not?	
Answer the Problem	☐ Be sure to give your answer on the previous page

 © 2005 Englefield & Associates, Inc.

Measurement
Multiple-Choice Practice Problem 14

14. Josh knows that 40 1" blocks cover the bottom of the box.

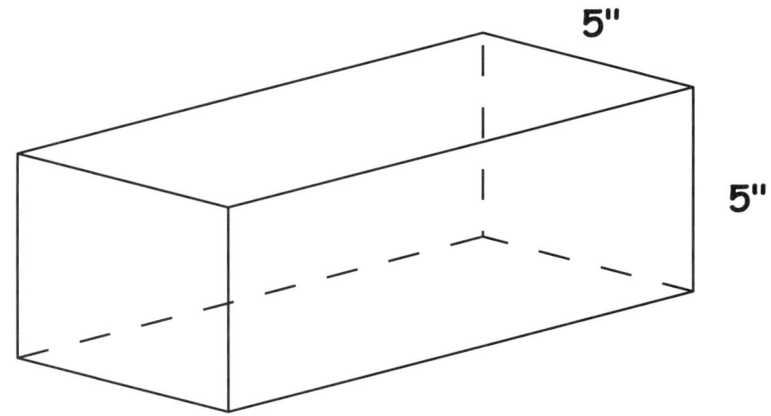

5"

5"

He needs to know how many blocks will fill the box. Three of the following equations will give him the correct answer. Which equation is incorrect?

○ A. V = 25 x 8

○ B. V = 8 x 5 x 5

○ C. V = 40 x 8

○ D. V = 40 x 5

Use the thinking map on the next page to solve the problem.
Fill in the circle next to the correct answer.
Mark only one answer.

Thinking Map

Read the Problem	☐ Read the Problem
Reread the Problem	☐ Reread the Problem
Write the important math vocabulary that tells you what to do.	
Reread the Problem	☐ Reread the Problem
What information do you have that you can use to solve the problem? Can you get clues from: ☐ The answer choices ☐ Pictures, charts, or graphs ☐ A problem you have solved before	
Reread the Problem	☐ Reread the Problem
Solve the problem. Use one or more: ☐ Act it out. ☐ Use manipulatives. You can: ☐ Do a calculation: addition, subtraction, multiplication, or division. ☐ Draw a picture, graph, or table. ☐ Set up an equation. ☐ Write a formula.	
Use words, pictures, or numbers to explain your answer.	
Does your answer make sense? Why or why not?	
Answer the Problem	☐ Be sure to give your answer on the previous page

Measurement
Multiple-Choice Practice Problem 15

15. Estimate the height of the tree to the nearest meter.

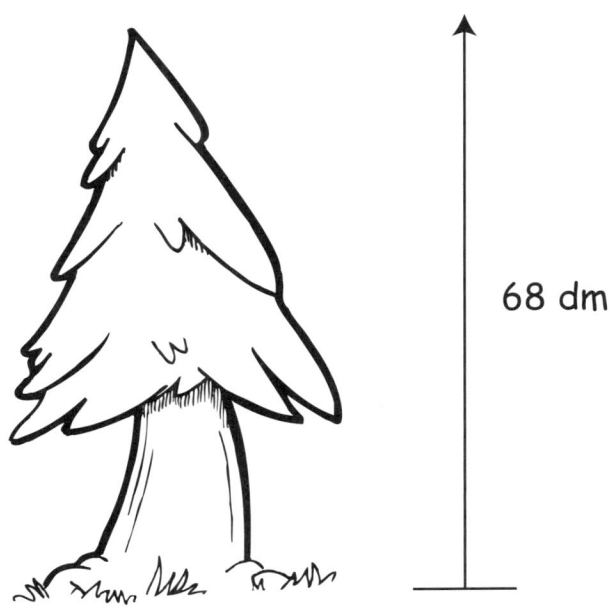

68 dm

○ A. 8 meters

○ B. 14 meters

○ C. 6 meters

○ D. 7 meters

Use the thinking map on the next page to solve the problem.
Fill in the circle next to the correct answer.
Mark only one answer.

DO NOT COPY

Thinking Map

Read the Problem	☐ Read the Problem
Reread the Problem	☐ Reread the Problem
Write the important math vocabulary that tells you what to do.	
Reread the Problem	☐ Reread the Problem
What information do you have that you can use to solve the problem? Can you get clues from: ☐ The answer choices ☐ Pictures, charts, or graphs ☐ A problem you have solved before	
Reread the Problem	☐ Reread the Problem
Solve the problem. Use one or more: ☐ Act it out. ☐ Use manipulatives. You can: ☐ Do a calculation: addition, subtraction, multiplication, or division. ☐ Draw a picture, graph, or table. ☐ Set up an equation. ☐ Write a formula.	
Use words, pictures, or numbers to explain your answer.	
Does your answer make sense? Why or why not?	
Answer the Problem	☐ Be sure to give your answer on the previous page

 © 2005 Englefield & Associates, Inc.

Measurement
Multiple-Choice Practice Problem 16

16. Marcy set her watch to the correct time on October 1. Marcy's watch doesn't keep perfect time; it gains two minutes each day. On October 30, she had to set her watch back one hour for the end of daylight savings time. How many minutes did Marcy have to set her watch back to get the correct time?

○ A. 30

○ B. 60

○ C. 0

○ D. 120

Use the thinking map on the next page to solve the problem.
Fill in the circle next to the correct answer.
Mark only one answer.

DO NOT COPY

Thinking Map

Read the Problem	☐ Read the Problem
Reread the Problem	☐ Reread the Problem
Write the important math vocabulary that tells you what to do.	
Reread the Problem	☐ Reread the Problem
What information do you have that you can use to solve the problem? Can you get clues from: ☐ The answer choices ☐ Pictures, charts, or graphs ☐ A problem you have solved before	
Reread the Problem	☐ Reread the Problem
Solve the problem. Use one or more: ☐ Act it out. ☐ Use manipulatives. You can: ☐ Do a calculation: addition, subtraction, multiplication, or division. ☐ Draw a picture, graph, or table. ☐ Set up an equation. ☐ Write a formula.	
Use words, pictures, or numbers to explain your answer.	
Does your answer make sense? Why or why not?	
Answer the Problem	☐ Be sure to give your answer on the previous page

Measurement
Multiple-Choice Practice Problem 17

17. Allison had 1 gallon of punch. She drank 1 cup. How much was left?

○ A. 4 qts, 1 cup

○ B. 3 qts, 1 pt, 1 cup

○ C. 3 qts, 2 pts, 2 cups

○ D. 3 qts, 1 pt, 2 cups

Use the thinking map on the next page to solve the problem.
Fill in the circle next to the correct answer.
Mark only one answer.

Thinking Map

Read the Problem	☐ Read the Problem
Reread the Problem	☐ Reread the Problem
Write the important math vocabulary that tells you what to do.	
Reread the Problem	☐ Reread the Problem
What information do you have that you can use to solve the problem? Can you get clues from: ☐ The answer choices ☐ Pictures, charts, or graphs ☐ A problem you have solved before	
Reread the Problem	☐ Reread the Problem
Solve the problem. Use one or more: ☐ Act it out. ☐ Use manipulatives. You can: ☐ Do a calculation: addition, subtraction, multiplication, or division. ☐ Draw a picture, graph, or table. ☐ Set up an equation. ☐ Write a formula.	
Use words, pictures, or numbers to explain your answer.	
Does your answer make sense? Why or why not?	
Answer the Problem	☐ Be sure to give your answer on the previous page

Model Problem 5:
Measurement
Short-Answer

5. Ray's weight is 3 times the weight of his sister. His father weighs twice Ray's weight. Their total weight is 400 pounds. How much does each person weigh?

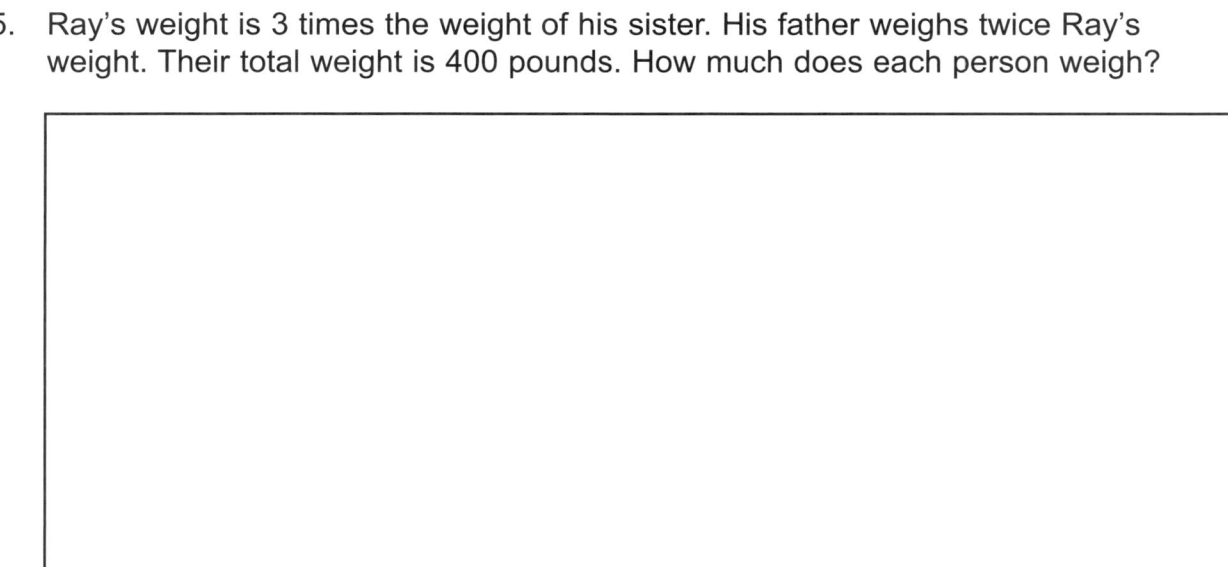

**Use the thinking map on the next page to solve the problem.
Write your answer in the box.**

Thinking Map

Read the Problem	☐ Read the Problem
Reread the Problem	☐ Reread the Problem
Write the important math vocabulary that tells you what to do.	
Reread the Problem	☐ Reread the Problem
What information do you have that you can use to solve the problem? Can you get clues from: ☐ The answer choices ☐ Pictures, charts, or graphs ☐ A problem you have solved before	
Reread the Problem	☐ Reread the Problem
Solve the problem. Use one or more: ☐ Act it out. ☐ Use manipulatives. You can: ☐ Do a calculation: addition, subtraction, multiplication, or division. ☐ Draw a picture, graph, or table. ☐ Set up an equation. ☐ Write a formula.	
Use words, pictures, or numbers to explain your answer.	
Does your answer make sense? Why or why not?	
Answer the Problem	☐ Be sure to give your answer on the previous page

One Way to Complete the Thinking Map

Read the Problem	☑ Read the Problem
Reread the Problem	☑ Reread the Problem
Write the important math vocabulary that tells you what to do.	3 times the weight twice the weight total is 400 lbs How much does each person weigh?
Reread the Problem	☑ Reread the Problem
What information do you have that you can use to solve the problem? Can you get clues from: ☑ The answer choices ☐ Pictures, charts, or graphs ☑ A problem you have solved before	Ray = 3 times his sister father = 2 times Ray total = 400 lbs
Reread the Problem	☑ Reread the Problem
Solve the problem. Use one or more: ☐ Act it out. ☐ Use manipulatives. You can: ☐ Do a calculation: addition, subtraction, multiplication, or division. ☐ Draw a picture, graph, or table. ☑ Set up an equation. ☐ Write a formula.	Sister = N lbs Ray = 3 x N lbs (3 times his sister) father = 2 x (3N) lbs (2 times Ray) Equation: $N + 3N + (2 \times (3N)) = 400$ $N + 3N + 6N = 400$ $10N = 40$
Use words, pictures, or numbers to explain your answer.	N = Sister = 40 lbs Ray = 3N = 3 x 40 = 120 lbs Father = 2 x 3N = 2 x 120 = 240 lbs
Does your answer make sense? Why or why not?	Yes—40 + 120 + 240 = 400. Each number represents a reasonable amount for a person to weigh.
Answer the Problem	☑ Be sure to give your answer on the previous page

Measurement
Short-Answer Practice Problem 18

18. Estimate which set of numbers has a mean that is closer to 78. Explain how you came up with your answer.

76, 75, 69, 81, 77, 79

76, 77, 78, 57, 82, 71

Use the thinking map on the next page to solve the problem.
Write your answer in the box.

Thinking Map

Read the Problem	☐ Read the Problem
Reread the Problem	☐ Reread the Problem
Write the important math vocabulary that tells you what to do.	
Reread the Problem	☐ Reread the Problem
What information do you have that you can use to solve the problem? Can you get clues from: ☐ The answer choices ☐ Pictures, charts, or graphs ☐ A problem you have solved before	
Reread the Problem	☐ Reread the Problem
Solve the problem. Use one or more: ☐ Act it out. ☐ Use manipulatives. You can: ☐ Do a calculation: addition, subtraction, multiplication, or division. ☐ Draw a picture, graph, or table. ☐ Set up an equation. ☐ Write a formula.	
Use words, pictures, or numbers to explain your answer.	
Does your answer make sense? Why or why not?	
Answer the Problem	☐ Be sure to give your answer on the previous page

Measurement
Short-Answer Practice Problem 19

19. Laddan grooms dogs at the pet store. She charges $30 for each grooming, and each dog takes 30 minutes to groom. She needs 15 minutes to get ready for the next dog. She works from 9:00 a.m. to 4:00 p.m. She gets 30 minutes every day for lunch. What is the maximum number of dogs she can groom in one day?

**Use the thinking map on the next page to solve the problem.
Write your answer in the box.**

DO NOT COPY © 2005 Englefield & Associates, Inc.

Thinking Map

Read the Problem	☐ Read the Problem
Reread the Problem	☐ Reread the Problem
Write the important math vocabulary that tells you what to do.	
Reread the Problem	☐ Reread the Problem
What information do you have that you can use to solve the problem? Can you get clues from: ☐ The answer choices ☐ Pictures, charts, or graphs ☐ A problem you have solved before	
Reread the Problem	☐ Reread the Problem
Solve the problem. Use one or more: ☐ Act it out. ☐ Use manipulatives. You can: ☐ Do a calculation: addition, subtraction, multiplication, or division. ☐ Draw a picture, graph, or table. ☐ Set up an equation. ☐ Write a formula.	
Use words, pictures, or numbers to explain your answer.	
Does your answer make sense? Why or why not?	
Answer the Problem	☐ Be sure to give your answer on the previous page

Model Problem 6:
Measurement
Extended-Response

6. Shelby started from home and rode her bike 4 blocks east, 6 blocks south, and 4 blocks west. She then turned north toward home and got a flat tire. She had to walk the rest of the way home. How many blocks did she walk?

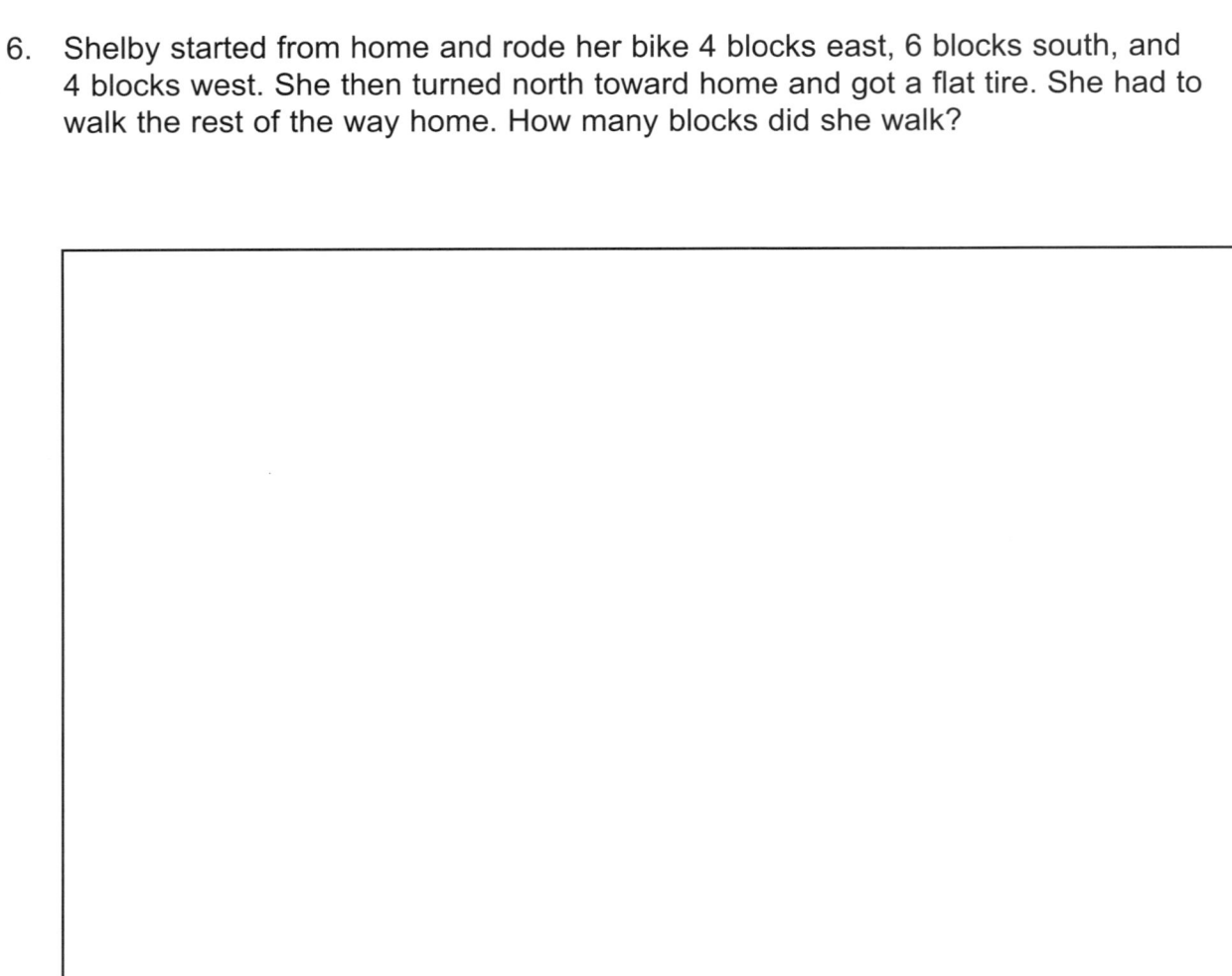

Use the thinking map on the next page to solve the problem.
Write your answer in the box.

Thinking Map

Read the Problem	☐ Read the Problem
Reread the Problem	☐ Reread the Problem
Write the important math vocabulary that tells you what to do.	
Reread the Problem	☐ Reread the Problem
What information do you have that you can use to solve the problem? Can you get clues from: ☐ The answer choices ☐ Pictures, charts, or graphs ☐ A problem you have solved before	
Reread the Problem	☐ Reread the Problem
Solve the problem. Use one or more: ☐ Act it out. ☐ Use manipulatives. You can: ☐ Do a calculation: addition, subtraction, multiplication, or division. ☐ Draw a picture, graph, or table. ☐ Set up an equation. ☐ Write a formula.	
Use words, pictures, or numbers to explain your answer.	
Does your answer make sense? Why or why not?	
Answer the Problem	☐ Be sure to give your answer on the previous page

One Way to Complete the Thinking Map

Read the Problem	☑ Read the Problem
Reread the Problem	☑ Reread the Problem
Write the important math vocabulary that tells you what to do.	Directions: north, south, east, west How many
Reread the Problem	☐ Reread the Problem
What information do you have that you can use to solve the problem? Can you get clues from: ☐ The answer choices ☐ Pictures, charts, or graphs ☑ A problem you have solved before	4 blocks east 6 blocks south 4 blocks west
Reread the Problem	☑ Reread the Problem
Solve the problem. Use one or more: ☐ Act it out. ☐ Use manipulatives. You can: ☐ Do a calculation: addition, subtraction, multiplication, or division. ☑ Draw a picture, graph, or table. ☑ Set up an equation. ☑ Write a formula.	home flat tire By drawing a diagram of her path, you can see that her path created a rectangle. The black line is her riding path. She rode 4 blocks east, 6 blocks south, and 4 blocks west.
Use words, pictures, or numbers to explain your answer.	Shelby walked 6 blocks. Distance she rode south equals the distance she walked home.
Does your answer make sense? Why or why not?	Yes. When you recognize that the path she rode created a rectangle, you can see that the distance is determined by the properties of a rectangle.
Answer the Problem	☑ Be sure to give your answer on the previous page

Measurement
Extended-Response Practice Problem 20

20. The perimeter of a rectangle is 36. How many different rectangles can you make that have a perimeter of 36?

Use the thinking map on the next page to solve the problem.
Write your answer in the box.

Thinking Map

Read the Problem	☐ Read the Problem
Reread the Problem	☐ Reread the Problem
Write the important math vocabulary that tells you what to do.	
Reread the Problem	☐ Reread the Problem
What information do you have that you can use to solve the problem? Can you get clues from: ☐ The answer choices ☐ Pictures, charts, or graphs ☐ A problem you have solved before	
Reread the Problem	☐ Reread the Problem
Solve the problem. Use one or more: ☐ Act it out. ☐ Use manipulatives. You can: ☐ Do a calculation: addition, subtraction, multiplication, or division. ☐ Draw a picture, graph, or table. ☐ Set up an equation. ☐ Write a formula.	
Use words, pictures, or numbers to explain your answer.	
Does your answer make sense? Why or why not?	
Answer the Problem	☐ Be sure to give your answer on the previous page

Chapter 3

Geometry

What is Geometry?

In Geometry, you will learn

- New vocabulary to describe circles, angle parts, and lines.

- To measure the degree of rotation of an angle.

- About negative numbers.

What does Geometry look like?

- You will use new terms, such as radius, diameter, circumference, parallel, and perpendicular.

- You will visualize to predict and describe the movement of objects and shapes.

- You will measure angles in your environment.

- You will find the difference between points on a graph with positive and negative numbers.

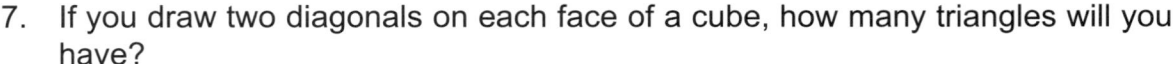

Model Problem 7:
Geometry
Multiple-Choice

7. If you draw two diagonals on each face of a cube, how many triangles will you have?

  ○ A. 16

  ○ B. 32

  ○ C. 24

  ○ D. 36

**Use the thinking map on the next page to solve the problem.
Fill in the circle next to the correct answer.
Mark only one answer.**

Thinking Map

Read the Problem	☐ Read the Problem
Reread the Problem	☐ Reread the Problem
Write the important math vocabulary that tells you what to do.	
Reread the Problem	☐ Reread the Problem
What information do you have that you can use to solve the problem? Can you get clues from: ☐ The answer choices ☐ Pictures, charts, or graphs ☐ A problem you have solved before	
Reread the Problem	☐ Reread the Problem
Solve the problem. Use one or more: ☐ Act it out. ☐ Use manipulatives. You can: ☐ Do a calculation: addition, subtraction, multiplication, or division. ☐ Draw a picture, graph, or table. ☐ Set up an equation. ☐ Write a formula.	
Use words, pictures, or numbers to explain your answer.	
Does your answer make sense? Why or why not?	
Answer the Problem	☐ Be sure to give your answer on the previous page

One Way to Complete the Thinking Map

Read the Problem	☑ Read the Problem
Reread the Problem	☑ Reread the Problem
Write the important math vocabulary that tells you what to do.	diagonals cube
Reread the Problem	☑ Reread the Problem
What information do you have that you can use to solve the problem? Can you get clues from: ☑ The answer choices ☐ Pictures, charts, or graphs ☑ A problem you have solved before	cube has 6 faces diagonal bisects a square from corner to corner
Reread the Problem	☑ Reread the Problem
Solve the problem. Use one or more: ☐ Act it out. ☐ Use manipulatives. You can: ☐ Do a calculation: addition, subtraction, multiplication, or division. ☑ Draw a picture, graph, or table. ☐ Set up an equation. ☐ Write a formula.	Cube has 6 faces 2 diagonals divide each face into 4 triangles 4 x 6 = 24
Use words, pictures, or numbers to explain your answer.	Each face has 4 triangles. A cube has 6 faces. 6 x 4 = 24 triangles. Answer = C
Does your answer make sense? Why or why not?	Yes; 6 faces x 4 triangles on each face = 24 triangles.
Answer the Problem	☑ Be sure to give your answer on the previous page

Geometry
Multiple-Choice Practice Problem 21

21. Juan wants to find a rug that will cover the largest area in his dormitory room. Which rug should he buy?

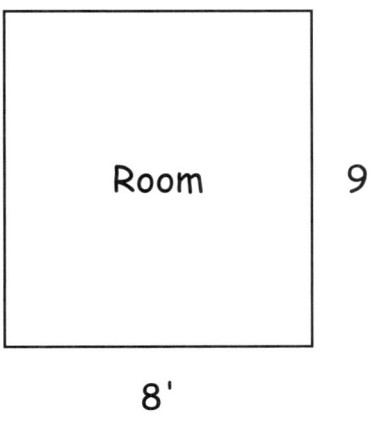

Room   9'

8'

○ A. 8' x 10'

○ B. 7' x 9'

○ C. $8\frac{1}{2}$' x 8'

○ D. 7.5' x 9'

Use the thinking map on the next page to solve the problem.
Fill in the circle next to the correct answer.
Mark only one answer.

DO NOT COPY

Thinking Map

Read the Problem	☐ Read the Problem
Reread the Problem	☐ Reread the Problem
Write the important math vocabulary that tells you what to do.	
Reread the Problem	☐ Reread the Problem
What information do you have that you can use to solve the problem? Can you get clues from: ☐ The answer choices ☐ Pictures, charts, or graphs ☐ A problem you have solved before	
Reread the Problem	☐ Reread the Problem
Solve the problem. Use one or more: ☐ Act it out. ☐ Use manipulatives. You can: ☐ Do a calculation: addition, subtraction, multiplication, or division. ☐ Draw a picture, graph, or table. ☐ Set up an equation. ☐ Write a formula.	
Use words, pictures, or numbers to explain your answer.	
Does your answer make sense? Why or why not?	
Answer the Problem	☐ Be sure to give your answer on the previous page

DO NOT COPY

Geometry
Multiple-Choice Practice Problem 22

22. Mr. Robb has a scale drawing of his new office. He wants to order carpet. How much carpet does he need?

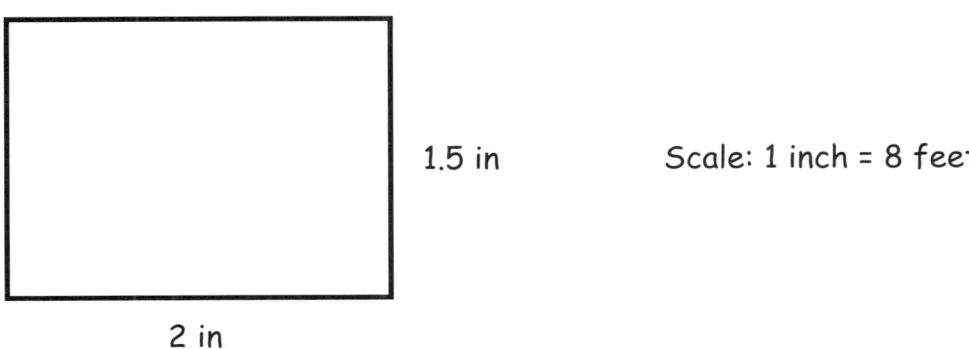

1.5 in   Scale: 1 inch = 8 feet

2 in

○ A. 24 square feet

○ B. 16 square feet

○ C. 192 square feet

○ D. 128 square feet

Use the thinking map on the next page to solve the problem.
Fill in the circle next to the correct answer.
Mark only one answer.

Thinking Map

Read the Problem	☐ Read the Problem
Reread the Problem	☐ Reread the Problem
Write the important math vocabulary that tells you what to do.	
Reread the Problem	☐ Reread the Problem
What information do you have that you can use to solve the problem? Can you get clues from: ☐ The answer choices ☐ Pictures, charts, or graphs ☐ A problem you have solved before	
Reread the Problem	☐ Reread the Problem
Solve the problem. Use one or more: ☐ Act it out. ☐ Use manipulatives. You can: ☐ Do a calculation: addition, subtraction, multiplication, or division. ☐ Draw a picture, graph, or table. ☐ Set up an equation. ☐ Write a formula.	
Use words, pictures, or numbers to explain your answer.	
Does your answer make sense? Why or why not?	
Answer the Problem	☐ Be sure to give your answer on the previous page

 © 2005 Englefield & Associates, Inc.

Geometry
Multiple-Choice Practice Problem 23

23. The school system wants to build a ball field halfway between the elementary school and the middle school. On the graph, find the midpoint where the ball field should be placed.

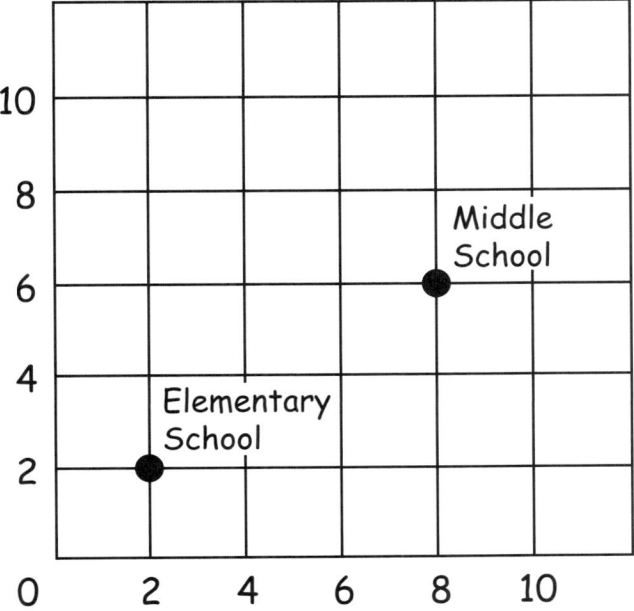

○ A. (5, 4)

○ B. (6, 4)

○ C. (4, 3)

○ D. (4, 4)

Use the thinking map on the next page to solve the problem.
Fill in the circle next to the correct answer.
Mark only one answer.

Thinking Map

Read the Problem	☐ Read the Problem
Reread the Problem	☐ Reread the Problem
Write the important math vocabulary that tells you what to do.	
Reread the Problem	☐ Reread the Problem
What information do you have that you can use to solve the problem? Can you get clues from: ☐ The answer choices ☐ Pictures, charts, or graphs ☐ A problem you have solved before	
Reread the Problem	☐ Reread the Problem
Solve the problem. Use one or more: ☐ Act it out. ☐ Use manipulatives. You can: ☐ Do a calculation: addition, subtraction, multiplication, or division. ☐ Draw a picture, graph, or table. ☐ Set up an equation. ☐ Write a formula.	
Use words, pictures, or numbers to explain your answer.	
Does your answer make sense? Why or why not?	
Answer the Problem	☐ Be sure to give your answer on the previous page

 © 2005 Englefield & Associates, Inc.

Geometry
Multiple-Choice Practice Problem 24

24. Three students drew the following nets for a triangular prism. Which student was correct?

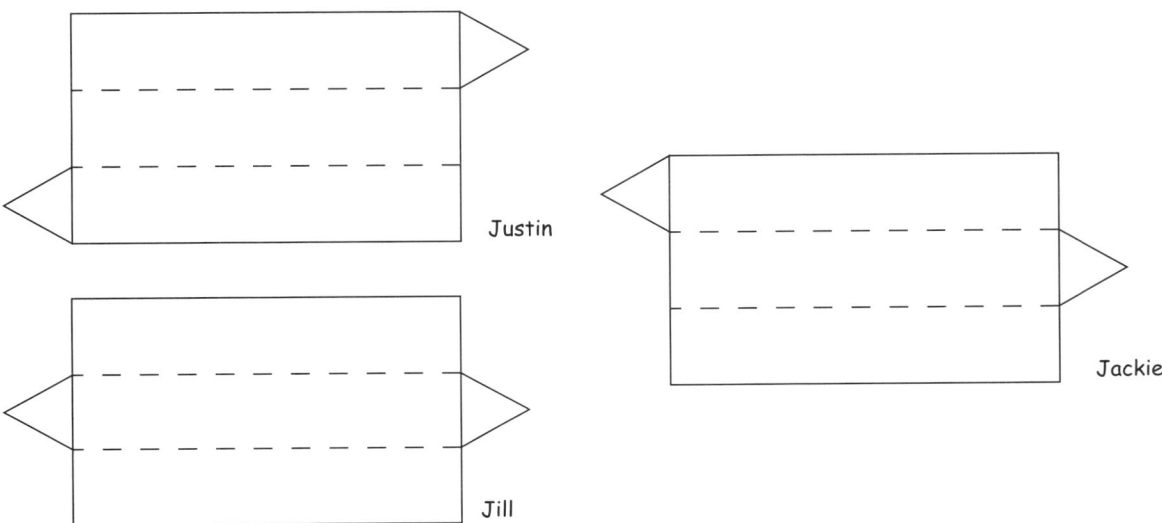

○ A. Justin

○ B. Jill

○ C. Jackie

○ D. All three students

**Use the thinking map on the next page to solve the problem.
Fill in the circle next to the correct answer.
Mark only one answer.**

Thinking Map

Read the Problem	☐ Read the Problem
Reread the Problem	☐ Reread the Problem
Write the important math vocabulary that tells you what to do.	
Reread the Problem	☐ Reread the Problem
What information do you have that you can use to solve the problem? Can you get clues from: ☐ The answer choices ☐ Pictures, charts, or graphs ☐ A problem you have solved before	
Reread the Problem	☐ Reread the Problem
Solve the problem. Use one or more: ☐ Act it out. ☐ Use manipulatives. You can: ☐ Do a calculation: addition, subtraction, multiplication, or division. ☐ Draw a picture, graph, or table. ☐ Set up an equation. ☐ Write a formula.	
Use words, pictures, or numbers to explain your answer.	
Does your answer make sense? Why or why not?	
Answer the Problem	☐ Be sure to give your answer on the previous page

Geometry
Multiple-Choice Practice Problem 25

25. Which one of the following statements could be true?

   ○ A. Acute angle plus acute angle equals 180º.

   ○ B. Acute angle plus obtuse angle equals 180º.

   ○ C. Right angle plus acute angle equals 180º.

   ○ D. Obtuse angle plus obtuse angle equals 180º.

**Use the thinking map on the next page to solve the problem.
Fill in the circle next to the correct answer.
Mark only one answer.**

Thinking Map

Read the Problem	☐ Read the Problem
Reread the Problem	☐ Reread the Problem
Write the important math vocabulary that tells you what to do.	
Reread the Problem	☐ Reread the Problem
What information do you have that you can use to solve the problem? Can you get clues from: ☐ The answer choices ☐ Pictures, charts, or graphs ☐ A problem you have solved before	
Reread the Problem	☐ Reread the Problem
Solve the problem. Use one or more: ☐ Act it out. ☐ Use manipulatives. You can: ☐ Do a calculation: addition, subtraction, multiplication, or division. ☐ Draw a picture, graph, or table. ☐ Set up an equation. ☐ Write a formula.	
Use words, pictures, or numbers to explain your answer.	
Does your answer make sense? Why or why not?	
Answer the Problem	☐ Be sure to give your answer on the previous page

Geometry
Multiple-Choice Practice Problem 26

26. Point I is the center of the circle below. Which statement is true about the circle ?

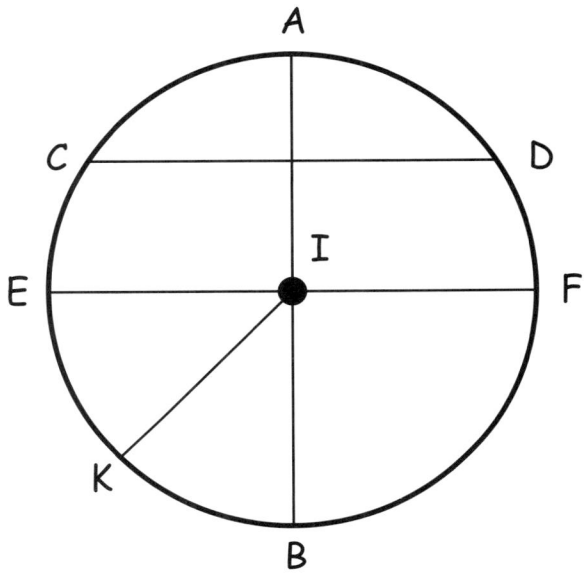

○ A. Segment CD is a diameter.

○ B. Figure EIK is a triangle.

○ C. Segment IF is a radius.

○ D. Segment IB is a chord.

**Use the thinking map on the next page to solve the problem.
Fill in the circle next to the correct answer.
Mark only one answer.**

Thinking Map

Read the Problem	☐ Read the Problem
Reread the Problem	☐ Reread the Problem
Write the important math vocabulary that tells you what to do.	
Reread the Problem	☐ Reread the Problem
What information do you have that you can use to solve the problem? Can you get clues from: ☐ The answer choices ☐ Pictures, charts, or graphs ☐ A problem you have solved before	
Reread the Problem	☐ Reread the Problem
Solve the problem. Use one or more: ☐ Act it out. ☐ Use manipulatives. You can: ☐ Do a calculation: addition, subtraction, multiplication, or division. ☐ Draw a picture, graph, or table. ☐ Set up an equation. ☐ Write a formula.	
Use words, pictures, or numbers to explain your answer.	
Does your answer make sense? Why or why not?	
Answer the Problem	☐ Be sure to give your answer on the previous page

Geometry
Multiple-Choice Practice Problem 27

27. Find the length of a side of a square with a perimeter of 34.

○ A. 8

○ B. $8\frac{1}{4}$

○ C. 7

○ D. $8\frac{1}{2}$

**Use the thinking map on the next page to solve the problem.
Fill in the circle next to the correct answer.
Mark only one answer.**

Thinking Map

Read the Problem	☐ Read the Problem
Reread the Problem	☐ Reread the Problem
Write the important math vocabulary that tells you what to do.	
Reread the Problem	☐ Reread the Problem
What information do you have that you can use to solve the problem? Can you get clues from: ☐ The answer choices ☐ Pictures, charts, or graphs ☐ A problem you have solved before	
Reread the Problem	☐ Reread the Problem
Solve the problem. Use one or more: ☐ Act it out. ☐ Use manipulatives. You can: ☐ Do a calculation: addition, subtraction, multiplication, or division. ☐ Draw a picture, graph, or table. ☐ Set up an equation. ☐ Write a formula.	
Use words, pictures, or numbers to explain your answer.	
Does your answer make sense? Why or why not?	
Answer the Problem	☐ Be sure to give your answer on the previous page

DO NOT COPY © 2005 Englefield & Associates, Inc.

Model Problem 8:
Geometry
Short-Answer

8. The perimeters of a square and a rectangle are both 32 feet. They are not the same figure. Which has the greater area?

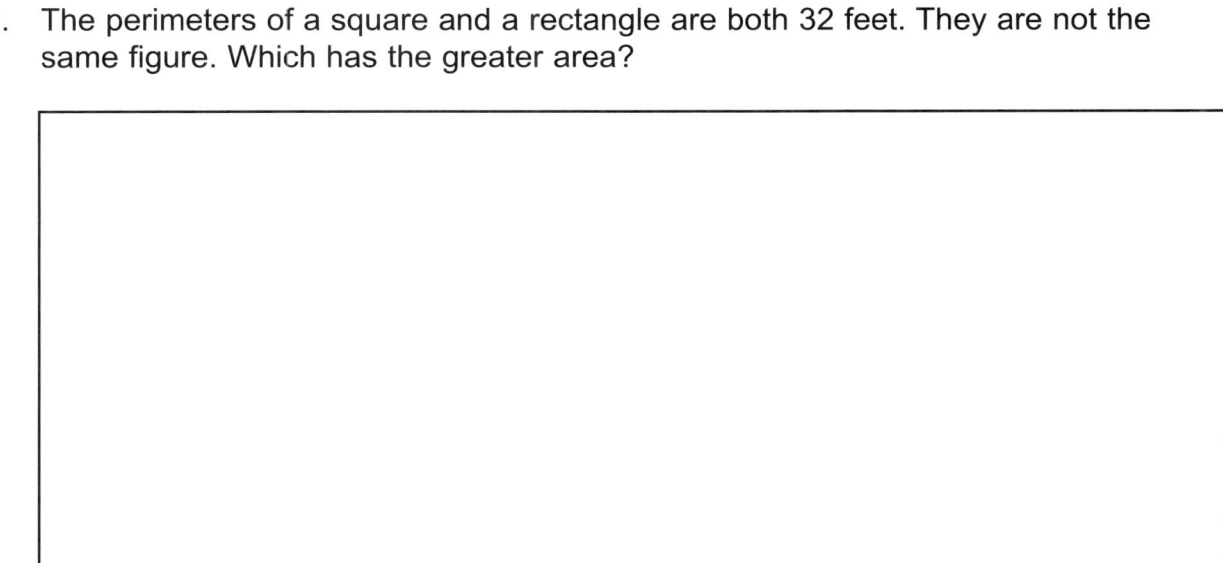

Use the thinking map on the next page to solve the problem.
Write your answer in the box.

Thinking Map

Read the Problem	☐ Read the Problem
Reread the Problem	☐ Reread the Problem
Write the important math vocabulary that tells you what to do.	
Reread the Problem	☐ Reread the Problem
What information do you have that you can use to solve the problem? Can you get clues from: ☐ The answer choices ☐ Pictures, charts, or graphs ☐ A problem you have solved before	
Reread the Problem	☐ Reread the Problem
Solve the problem. Use one or more: ☐ Act it out. ☐ Use manipulatives. **You can:** ☐ Do a calculation: addition, subtraction, multiplication, or division. ☐ Draw a picture, graph, or table. ☐ Set up an equation. ☐ Write a formula.	
Use words, pictures, or numbers to explain your answer.	
Does your answer make sense? Why or why not?	
Answer the Problem	☐ Be sure to give your answer on the previous page

One Way to Complete the Thinking Map

Read the Problem	✓ Read the Problem
Reread the Problem	✓ Reread the Problem
Write the important math vocabulary that tells you what to do.	perimeter of square perimeter of rectangle greater area
Reread the Problem	✓ Reread the Problem
What information do you have that you can use to solve the problem? Can you get clues from: ☐ The answer choices ☐ Pictures, charts, or graphs ✓ A problem you have solved before	P of sq. = S x 4 A of sq. = S^2 P of rec. = ($L + W$) x 2 A of rec. = L x W Perimeter of square = 32 Perimeter of rectangle = 32
Reread the Problem	✓ Reread the Problem

Solve the problem. Use one or more:
☐ Act it out.
☐ Use manipulatives.

You can:
☐ Do a calculation: addition, subtraction, multiplication, or division.
✓ Draw a picture, graph, or table.
☐ Set up an equation.
☐ Write a formula.

Side L	+	Side W	Per.	Area
8		8	32	64
7		9	32	63
6		10	32	60
5		11	32	55

Use words, pictures, or numbers to explain your answer.	The area of a square is greater than the area of a rectangle with the same perimeter.
Does your answer make sense? Why or why not?	Yes; the longer the side of a rectangle, the smaller the area. The closer the length and width of the rectangle are to being the same, the greater the area.
Answer the Problem	✓ Be sure to give your answer on the previous page

Geometry
Short-Answer Practice Problem 28

28. The area of a rhombus is 121 sq cm. What is the length of each side? Explain your answer.

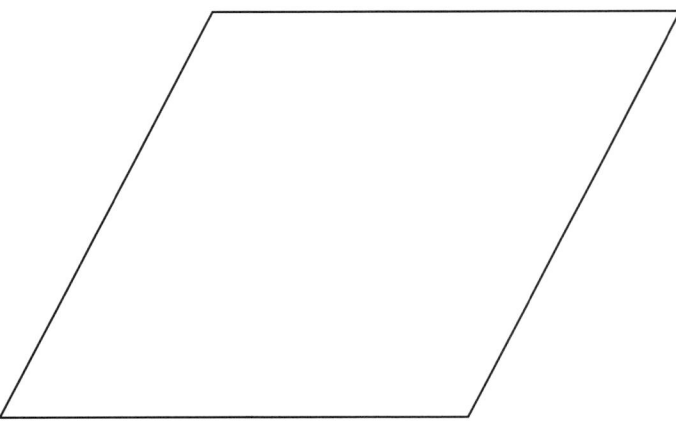

Use the thinking map on the next page to solve the problem.
Write your answer in the box.

 © 2005 Englefield & Associates, Inc.

Thinking Map

Read the Problem	☐ Read the Problem
Reread the Problem	☐ Reread the Problem
Write the important math vocabulary that tells you what to do.	
Reread the Problem	☐ Reread the Problem
What information do you have that you can use to solve the problem? Can you get clues from: ☐ The answer choices ☐ Pictures, charts, or graphs ☐ A problem you have solved before	
Reread the Problem	☐ Reread the Problem
Solve the problem. Use one or more: ☐ Act it out. ☐ Use manipulatives. You can: ☐ Do a calculation: addition, subtraction, multiplication, or division. ☐ Draw a picture, graph, or table. ☐ Set up an equation. ☐ Write a formula.	
Use words, pictures, or numbers to explain your answer.	
Does your answer make sense? Why or why not?	
Answer the Problem	☐ Be sure to give your answer on the previous page

Geometry
Short-Answer Practice Problem 29

29. A movie begins at 2:45 p.m. and lasts 1 hour and 40 minutes. It takes Julian 20 minutes to walk to the theater. At what time will he return home from the movie?

**Use the thinking map on the next page to solve the problem.
Write your answer in the box.**

DO NOT COPY © 2005 Englefield & Associates, Inc.

Thinking Map

Read the Problem	☐ Read the Problem
Reread the Problem	☐ Reread the Problem
Write the important math vocabulary that tells you what to do.	
Reread the Problem	☐ Reread the Problem
What information do you have that you can use to solve the problem? Can you get clues from: ☐ The answer choices ☐ Pictures, charts, or graphs ☐ A problem you have solved before	
Reread the Problem	☐ Reread the Problem
Solve the problem. Use one or more: ☐ Act it out. ☐ Use manipulatives. You can: ☐ Do a calculation: addition, subtraction, multiplication, or division. ☐ Draw a picture, graph, or table. ☐ Set up an equation. ☐ Write a formula.	
Use words, pictures, or numbers to explain your answer.	
Does your answer make sense? Why or why not?	
Answer the Problem	☐ Be sure to give your answer on the previous page

Model Problem 9:
Geometry
Extended-Response

9. Sammy wants to fence in his back yard. He knows the area and the perimeter, but he needs to know the length of each side. He knows the length of one side is 10 feet. The area of A = 30 square feet, and the area of B = 48 square feet. The perimeter is 44 feet.

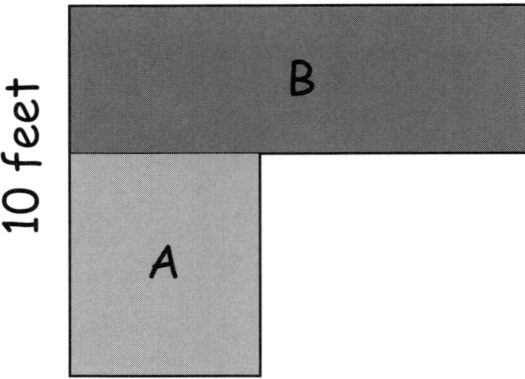

10 feet

B

A

**Use the thinking map on the next page to solve the problem.
Write your answer in the box.**

Thinking Map

Read the Problem	☐ Read the Problem
Reread the Problem	☐ Reread the Problem
Write the important math vocabulary that tells you what to do.	
Reread the Problem	☐ Reread the Problem
What information do you have that you can use to solve the problem? Can you get clues from: ☐ The answer choices ☐ Pictures, charts, or graphs ☐ A problem you have solved before	
Reread the Problem	☐ Reread the Problem
Solve the problem. Use one or more: ☐ Act it out. ☐ Use manipulatives. You can: ☐ Do a calculation: addition, subtraction, multiplication, or division. ☐ Draw a picture, graph, or table. ☐ Set up an equation. ☐ Write a formula.	
Use words, pictures, or numbers to explain your answer.	
Does your answer make sense? Why or why not?	
Answer the Problem	☐ Be sure to give your answer on the previous page

One Way to Complete the Thinking Map

Read the Problem	☑ Read the Problem
Reread the Problem	☑ Reread the Problem
Write the important math vocabulary that tells you what to do.	area perimeter length of sides
Reread the Problem	☑ Reread the Problem
What information do you have that you can use to solve the problem? Can you get clues from: ☐ The answer choices ☐ Pictures, charts, or graphs ☐ A problem you have solved before	 10 ft = 1 side Area A = 30 Area B = 48 Perimeter = 44
Reread the Problem	☑ Reread the Problem
Solve the problem. Use one or more: ☐ Act it out. ☐ Use manipulatives. You can: ☑ Do a calculation: addition, subtraction, multiplication, or division. ☑ Draw a picture, graph, or table. ☐ Set up an equation. ☐ Write a formula.	Copying the figure onto grid paper may help. Per. = 44; 1 side = 10 $10 + 10 + N + N = 44$ $44 - 20 = 24 = 2$ sides $24 \div 2 = 12$ long side = 12 If area B = 48 and side of B = 12 $48 = 12 \times N$; $N = 48 \div 12 = 4$; side of B = 4 If side of B = 4, side of A = $10 - 4 = 6$ Area of A = 30; $6 \times N = 30$; $N = 5$; side = 5
Use words, pictures, or numbers to explain your answer.	
Does your answer make sense? Why or why not?	Yes; add together lengths of sides: $10 + 12 + 4 + 7 + 6 + 5 = 44$ = Perimeter.
Answer the Problem	☑ Be sure to give your answer on the previous page

Geometry
Extended-Response Practice Problem 30

30. Tell whether each statement below is true or false. Explain your answer.

   A. A right triangle can be a scalene triangle.

   B. An equilateral triangle can be an obtuse triangle.

   C. An acute triangle can be a right triangle.

   D. An equilateral triangle can be an isosceles triangle.

**Use the thinking map on the next page to solve the problem.
Write your answer in the box.**

Thinking Map

Read the Problem	☐ Read the Problem
Reread the Problem	☐ Reread the Problem
Write the important math vocabulary that tells you what to do.	
Reread the Problem	☐ Reread the Problem
What information do you have that you can use to solve the problem? Can you get clues from: ☐ The answer choices ☐ Pictures, charts, or graphs ☐ A problem you have solved before	
Reread the Problem	☐ Reread the Problem
Solve the problem. Use one or more: ☐ Act it out. ☐ Use manipulatives. You can: ☐ Do a calculation: addition, subtraction, multiplication, or division. ☐ Draw a picture, graph, or table. ☐ Set up an equation. ☐ Write a formula.	
Use words, pictures, or numbers to explain your answer.	
Does your answer make sense? Why or why not?	
Answer the Problem	☐ Be sure to give your answer on the previous page

Chapter 4

Algebra

What is Algebra?

Algebra is important for the mathematics that you will study later in school. This year, you will learn the following about algebra:

- You will be asked to analyze patterns using words, tables, and graphs.
- You will learn about variables as unknown quantities using symbols such as boxes, *x*'s, or *n*'s.
- You will write equations.
- You will see how change affects patterns that you observe.

What does Algebra look like?

- You will describe patterns and represent the patterns using words, tables, or graphs.
- You will work with variables as unknown quantities.
- You will develop different strategies to solve multiplication problems.
- You will use real-world examples to make predictions and to discover that sometimes what actually happens does not match your prediction.

Model Problem 10:
Algebra
Multiple-Choice

10. Three children have matchbox car collections. Jack has 15 more cars than Tim. Tim has one-fourth as many cars as Chris. If Chris has 20 cars, how many cars do Tim and Jack have together?

○ A. 15

○ B. 25

○ C. 20

○ D. 40

Use the thinking map on the next page to solve the problem.
Fill in the circle next to the correct answer.
Mark only one answer.

Thinking Map

Read the Problem	☐ Read the Problem
Reread the Problem	☐ Reread the Problem
Write the important math vocabulary that tells you what to do.	
Reread the Problem	☐ Reread the Problem
What information do you have that you can use to solve the problem? Can you get clues from: ☐ The answer choices ☐ Pictures, charts, or graphs ☐ A problem you have solved before	
Reread the Problem	☐ Reread the Problem
Solve the problem. Use one or more: ☐ Act it out. ☐ Use manipulatives. You can: ☐ Do a calculation: addition, subtraction, multiplication, or division. ☐ Draw a picture, graph, or table. ☐ Set up an equation. ☐ Write a formula.	
Use words, pictures, or numbers to explain your answer.	
Does your answer make sense? Why or why not?	
Answer the Problem	☐ Be sure to give your answer on the previous page

One Way to Complete the Thinking Map

Read the Problem	☑ Read the Problem
Reread the Problem	☑ Reread the Problem
Write the important math vocabulary that tells you what to do.	How many cars do Tim and Jack have together?
Reread the Problem	☑ Reread the Problem
What information do you have that you can use to solve the problem? Can you get clues from: ☐ The answer choices ☐ Pictures, charts, or graphs ☑ A problem you have solved before	Jack has 15 more than Tim Tim has $\frac{1}{4}$ as many as Chris Chris has 20 Tim + Jack = ☐
Reread the Problem	☑ Reread the Problem
Solve the problem. Use one or more: ☐ Act it out. ☐ Use manipulatives. You can: ☑ Do a calculation: addition, subtraction, multiplication, or division. ☐ Draw a picture, graph, or table. ☑ Set up an equation. ☐ Write a formula.	Chris has 20 Tim has $\frac{1}{4}$ of 20; Tim has $20 \div 4 = 5$ Jack has 15 more than Tim (5) Jack has 20 $T + J = $ ☐ $5 + 20 = 25$
Use words, pictures, or numbers to explain your answer.	Write in equations: $T = 20 \div 4 \quad T = 5$ $J = 15 + 5 \quad J = 20$ $T + J = N$ $5 + 20 = 25; N = 25$ Answer B is correct.
Does your answer make sense? Why or why not?	Yes, because I can check and see that 5 is one-fourth of 20, and 20 is 15 more than 5.
Answer the Problem	☑ Be sure to give your answer on the previous page

Algebra
Multiple-Choice Practice Problem 31

31. Identify the function that makes this pattern.

$$\frac{1}{8}, \frac{1}{4}, \frac{3}{8}, \frac{1}{2}, \frac{5}{8}, \frac{3}{4}, \frac{7}{8}, 1$$

○ A. Add $\frac{1}{4}$

○ B. Subtract $\frac{1}{8}$

○ C. Add $\frac{1}{8}$

○ D. Add $\frac{2}{8}$

Use the thinking map on the next page to solve the problem.
Fill in the circle next to the correct answer.
Mark only one answer.

DO NOT COPY

Thinking Map

Read the Problem	☐ Read the Problem
Reread the Problem	☐ Reread the Problem
Write the important math vocabulary that tells you what to do.	
Reread the Problem	☐ Reread the Problem
What information do you have that you can use to solve the problem? Can you get clues from: ☐ The answer choices ☐ Pictures, charts, or graphs ☐ A problem you have solved before	
Reread the Problem	☐ Reread the Problem
Solve the problem. Use one or more: ☐ Act it out. ☐ Use manipulatives. You can: ☐ Do a calculation: addition, subtraction, multiplication, or division. ☐ Draw a picture, graph, or table. ☐ Set up an equation. ☐ Write a formula.	
Use words, pictures, or numbers to explain your answer.	
Does your answer make sense? Why or why not?	
Answer the Problem	☐ Be sure to give your answer on the previous page

Algebra
Multiple-Choice Practice Problem 32

32. You are saving for a CD player. It will cost $59.00. If you save $3.50 per week for the next five weeks, you will have enough. How much money have you saved? Which equation can help you find the answer?

   ○ A. $N = 3.50 \times 5$

   ○ B. $N = 59.00 + (3.50 \times 5)$

   ○ C. $N = 59.00 - (5 \times 3.50)$

   ○ D. $N = 5 \times (59.00 - 3.50)$

Use the thinking map on the next page to solve the problem.
Fill in the circle next to the correct answer.
Mark only one answer.

Thinking Map

Read the Problem	☐ Read the Problem
Reread the Problem	☐ Reread the Problem
Write the important math vocabulary that tells you what to do.	
Reread the Problem	☐ Reread the Problem
What information do you have that you can use to solve the problem? Can you get clues from: ☐ The answer choices ☐ Pictures, charts, or graphs ☐ A problem you have solved before	
Reread the Problem	☐ Reread the Problem
Solve the problem. Use one or more: ☐ Act it out. ☐ Use manipulatives. You can: ☐ Do a calculation: addition, subtraction, multiplication, or division. ☐ Draw a picture, graph, or table. ☐ Set up an equation. ☐ Write a formula.	
Use words, pictures, or numbers to explain your answer.	
Does your answer make sense? Why or why not?	
Answer the Problem	☐ Be sure to give your answer on the previous page

Algebra
Multiple-Choice Practice Problem 33

33. Dan brought 148 baseball cards to school. He traded with his friends at recess. He traded 2 for 1 so he could get the special cards he wanted. At the end of the day, he had 112 of his original cards left. Which equation shows how many new cards Dan has?

   ○ A. $C = 148 - 2 + 112$

   ○ B. $C = (148 + 112) - 2$

   ○ C. $C = 2 \times (148 - 112)$

   ○ D. $C = (148 - 112) \div 2$

Use the thinking map on the next page to solve the problem.
Fill in the circle next to the correct answer.
Mark only one answer.

Thinking Map

Read the Problem	☐ Read the Problem
Reread the Problem	☐ Reread the Problem
Write the important math vocabulary that tells you what to do.	
Reread the Problem	☐ Reread the Problem
What information do you have that you can use to solve the problem? Can you get clues from: ☐ The answer choices ☐ Pictures, charts, or graphs ☐ A problem you have solved before	
Reread the Problem	☐ Reread the Problem
Solve the problem. Use one or more: ☐ Act it out. ☐ Use manipulatives. You can: ☐ Do a calculation: addition, subtraction, multiplication, or division. ☐ Draw a picture, graph, or table. ☐ Set up an equation. ☐ Write a formula.	
Use words, pictures, or numbers to explain your answer.	
Does your answer make sense? Why or why not?	
Answer the Problem	☐ Be sure to give your answer on the previous page

DO NOT COPY

Algebra
Multiple-Choice Practice Problem 34

34. Carrie bought 2 books. The first book was full price, and the second book, of equal value, was on sale at half price. She spent $18. How much did she pay for each book? Which equation can help you solve this problem?

    ○ A. $2n = \$18.00$

    ○ B. $n \div 2 = 18$

    ○ C. $n + (n \div 2) = 18$

    ○ D. $n - 18 = 2$

**Use the thinking map on the next page to solve the problem.
Fill in the circle next to the correct answer.
Mark only one answer.**

Thinking Map

Read the Problem	☐ Read the Problem
Reread the Problem	☐ Reread the Problem
Write the important math vocabulary that tells you what to do.	
Reread the Problem	☐ Reread the Problem
What information do you have that you can use to solve the problem? Can you get clues from: ☐ The answer choices ☐ Pictures, charts, or graphs ☐ A problem you have solved before	
Reread the Problem	☐ Reread the Problem
Solve the problem. Use one or more: ☐ Act it out. ☐ Use manipulatives. **You can:** ☐ Do a calculation: addition, subtraction, multiplication, or division. ☐ Draw a picture, graph, or table. ☐ Set up an equation. ☐ Write a formula.	
Use words, pictures, or numbers to explain your answer.	
Does your answer make sense? Why or why not?	
Answer the Problem	☐ Be sure to give your answer on the previous page

DO NOT COPY

Algebra
Multiple-Choice Practice Problem 35

35. Jim's bus ride to and from school is 40 minutes total. He rode the bus 160 minutes this week. How many days was he absent?

○ A. 2

○ B. 1

○ C. 0

○ D. Not enough information is provided.

**Use the thinking map on the next page to solve the problem.
Fill in the circle next to the correct answer.
Mark only one answer.**

Thinking Map

Read the Problem	☐ Read the Problem
Reread the Problem	☐ Reread the Problem
Write the important math vocabulary that tells you what to do.	
Reread the Problem	☐ Reread the Problem
What information do you have that you can use to solve the problem? Can you get clues from: ☐ The answer choices ☐ Pictures, charts, or graphs ☐ A problem you have solved before	
Reread the Problem	☐ Reread the Problem
Solve the problem. Use one or more: ☐ Act it out. ☐ Use manipulatives. You can: ☐ Do a calculation: addition, subtraction, multiplication, or division. ☐ Draw a picture, graph, or table. ☐ Set up an equation. ☐ Write a formula.	
Use words, pictures, or numbers to explain your answer.	
Does your answer make sense? Why or why not?	
Answer the Problem	☐ Be sure to give your answer on the previous page

Algebra
Multiple-Choice Practice Problem 36

36. Bob charges $\frac{1}{4}$ less than his sister charges to cut the grass. His sister charges $24 per lawn and made $72 this week. Bob cut the same number of lawns this week as his sister did. How much did Bob make?

- ○ A. $48.00
- ○ B. $18.00
- ○ C. $96.00
- ○ D. $54.00

Use the thinking map on the next page to solve the problem.
Fill in the circle next to the correct answer.
Mark only one answer.

Thinking Map

Read the Problem	☐ Read the Problem
Reread the Problem	☐ Reread the Problem
Write the important math vocabulary that tells you what to do.	
Reread the Problem	☐ Reread the Problem
What information do you have that you can use to solve the problem? Can you get clues from: ☐ The answer choices ☐ Pictures, charts, or graphs ☐ A problem you have solved before	
Reread the Problem	☐ Reread the Problem
Solve the problem. Use one or more: ☐ Act it out. ☐ Use manipulatives. You can: ☐ Do a calculation: addition, subtraction, multiplication, or division. ☐ Draw a picture, graph, or table. ☐ Set up an equation. ☐ Write a formula.	
Use words, pictures, or numbers to explain your answer.	
Does your answer make sense? Why or why not?	
Answer the Problem	☐ Be sure to give your answer on the previous page

Algebra
Multiple-Choice Practice Problem 37

37. Mollie needed 16 favors for her birthday party. Play make-up kits cost $1.95 each. Mollie has $25.98 in her bank. Which equation will find how much more money she needs to buy 16 kits?

- ○ A. $M = \$1.95 \times 16$
- ○ B. $M = \$25.98 - 16$
- ○ C. $M = (16 \times \$1.95) - \$25.98$
- ○ D. $M = \$25.98 + \$1.95$

**Use the thinking map on the next page to solve the problem.
Fill in the circle next to the correct answer.
Mark only one answer.**

DO NOT COPY

Thinking Map

Read the Problem	☐ Read the Problem
Reread the Problem	☐ Reread the Problem
Write the important math vocabulary that tells you what to do.	
Reread the Problem	☐ Reread the Problem
What information do you have that you can use to solve the problem? Can you get clues from: ☐ The answer choices ☐ Pictures, charts, or graphs ☐ A problem you have solved before	
Reread the Problem	☐ Reread the Problem
Solve the problem. Use one or more: ☐ Act it out. ☐ Use manipulatives. You can: ☐ Do a calculation: addition, subtraction, multiplication, or division. ☐ Draw a picture, graph, or table. ☐ Set up an equation. ☐ Write a formula.	
Use words, pictures, or numbers to explain your answer.	
Does your answer make sense? Why or why not?	
Answer the Problem	☐ Be sure to give your answer on the previous page

DO NOT COPY

Model Problem 11:
Algebra
Short-Answer

11. Susan and her cousin were selling cookies to the neighborhood children after school. Susan bet her cousin that she could make twice as much money if she sold the cookies at a sale price of three for the price of two. If her cousin sold 15 cookies at $0.20 each, how many cookies did Susan need to sell to win her bet?

**Use the thinking map on the next page to solve the problem.
Write your answer in the box.**

Thinking Map

Read the Problem	☐ Read the Problem
Reread the Problem	☐ Reread the Problem
Write the important math vocabulary that tells you what to do.	
Reread the Problem	☐ Reread the Problem
What information do you have that you can use to solve the problem? Can you get clues from: ☐ The answer choices ☐ Pictures, charts, or graphs ☐ A problem you have solved before	
Reread the Problem	☐ Reread the Problem
Solve the problem. Use one or more: ☐ Act it out. ☐ Use manipulatives. You can: ☐ Do a calculation: addition, subtraction, multiplication, or division. ☐ Draw a picture, graph, or table. ☐ Set up an equation. ☐ Write a formula.	
Use words, pictures, or numbers to explain your answer.	
Does your answer make sense? Why or why not?	
Answer the Problem	☐ Be sure to give your answer on the previous page

One Way to Complete the Thinking Map

Read the Problem	☑ Read the Problem
Reread the Problem	☑ Reread the Problem
Write the important math vocabulary that tells you what to do.	How many did Susan have to sell to win the bet?
Reread the Problem	☑ Reread the Problem
What information do you have that you can use to solve the problem? Can you get clues from: ☐ The answer choices ☐ Pictures, charts, or graphs ☑ A problem you have solved before	Susan sold 3 cookies for $0.40 Cousin sold 15 at $0.20 each
Reread the Problem	☑ Reread the Problem
Solve the problem. Use one or more: ☐ Act it out. ☐ Use manipulatives. You can: ☑ Do a calculation: addition, subtraction, multiplication, or division. ☑ Draw a picture, graph, or table. ☑ Set up an equation. ☐ Write a formula.	Cousin: 15 x .20 = 3.00 Susan: $(N \div 3)$ x .40 = money earned 45 ÷ 3 = 15; 15 x .40 = 6.00 Susan: $(N \div 3)$ x .40 = cost (6 ÷ 3) x .40 = .80 (9 ÷ 3) x .40 = 1.20 (24 ÷ 3) x .40 = 3.20 (45 ÷ 3) x .40 = 6.00
Use words, pictures, or numbers to explain your answer.	Susan had to sell 45 cookies to make twice as much as her cousin. In order to win the bet, she had to sell 45 cookies.
Does your answer make sense? Why or why not?	Yes—the lower the price of the cookie, the more cookies have to be sold to earn the same amount.
Answer the Problem	☑ Be sure to give your answer on the previous page

Algebra
Short-Answer Practice Problem 38

38. Mark and Susy picked apples at the fruit farm. Susy picked three times as many as Mark. If Susy picked 36 apples, how many did Mark pick? How many apples did the two of them pick in all? Write an equation to solve each part of the problem.

**Use the thinking map on the next page to solve the problem.
Write your answer in the box.**

DO NOT COPY

Thinking Map

Read the Problem	☐ Read the Problem
Reread the Problem	☐ Reread the Problem
Write the important math vocabulary that tells you what to do.	
Reread the Problem	☐ Reread the Problem
What information do you have that you can use to solve the problem? Can you get clues from: ☐ The answer choices ☐ Pictures, charts, or graphs ☐ A problem you have solved before	
Reread the Problem	☐ Reread the Problem
Solve the problem. Use one or more: ☐ Act it out. ☐ Use manipulatives. You can: ☐ Do a calculation: addition, subtraction, multiplication, or division. ☐ Draw a picture, graph, or table. ☐ Set up an equation. ☐ Write a formula.	
Use words, pictures, or numbers to explain your answer.	
Does your answer make sense? Why or why not?	
Answer the Problem	☐ Be sure to give your answer on the previous page

Algebra
Short-Answer Practice Problem 39

39. A recipe for chocolate chip cookies calls for 12 oz of chocolate chips. Sharon wants to double the recipe. Sharon's mother has a large 36 oz bag of chocolate chips. How many ounces of chips does Sharon need? How can Sharon measure the amount she needs from the large bag?

**Use the thinking map on the next page to solve the problem.
Write your answer in the box.**

DO NOT COPY

Thinking Map

Read the Problem	☐ Read the Problem
Reread the Problem	☐ Reread the Problem
Write the important math vocabulary that tells you what to do.	
Reread the Problem	☐ Reread the Problem
What information do you have that you can use to solve the problem? Can you get clues from: ☐ The answer choices ☐ Pictures, charts, or graphs ☐ A problem you have solved before	
Reread the Problem	☐ Reread the Problem
Solve the problem. Use one or more: ☐ Act it out. ☐ Use manipulatives. **You can:** ☐ Do a calculation: addition, subtraction, multiplication, or division. ☐ Draw a picture, graph, or table. ☐ Set up an equation. ☐ Write a formula.	
Use words, pictures, or numbers to explain your answer.	
Does your answer make sense? Why or why not?	
Answer the Problem	☐ Be sure to give your answer on the previous page

Model Problem 12: Algebra Extended-Response

12. Students are selling candy bars at recess for a fundraiser. The number Beth sold is equal to the sum of the number Bob sold and the number Robin sold. Robin sold 2 more than Bob. Carmen sold the same number as José, and their total was the same as the number Beth sold. The total number sold was 24. How many candy bars did each student sell?

Use the thinking map on the next page to solve the problem.
Write your answer in the box.

DO NOT COPY

Thinking Map

Read the Problem	☐ Read the Problem
Reread the Problem	☐ Reread the Problem
Write the important math vocabulary that tells you what to do.	
Reread the Problem	☐ Reread the Problem
What information do you have that you can use to solve the problem? Can you get clues from: ☐ The answer choices ☐ Pictures, charts, or graphs ☐ A problem you have solved before	
Reread the Problem	☐ Reread the Problem
Solve the problem. Use one or more: ☐ Act it out. ☐ Use manipulatives. You can: ☐ Do a calculation: addition, subtraction, multiplication, or division. ☐ Draw a picture, graph, or table. ☐ Set up an equation. ☐ Write a formula.	
Use words, pictures, or numbers to explain your answer.	
Does your answer make sense? Why or why not?	
Answer the Problem	☐ Be sure to give your answer on the previous page

One Way to Complete the Thinking Map

Read the Problem	☑ Read the Problem
Reread the Problem	☑ Reread the Problem
Write the important math vocabulary that tells you what to do.	How many did each student sell?
Reread the Problem	☑ Reread the Problem
What information do you have that you can use to solve the problem? Can you get clues from: ☐ The answer choices ☐ Pictures, charts, or graphs ☐ A problem you have solved before	Robin = Bob + 2 Beth = Bob + Robin Carmen = José Carmen + José = Beth Total = 24
Reread the Problem	☑ Reread the Problem
Solve the problem. Use one or more: ☐ Act it out. ☐ Use manipulatives. You can: ☐ Do a calculation: addition, subtraction, multiplication, or division. ☑ Draw a picture, graph, or table. ☐ Set up an equation. ☐ Write a formula.	Two ways to solve: guess & check, or write an equation Bob = _____; Robin = Bob + 2 Beth = Robin + Bob Carmen & José = Beth ÷ 2 If Bob = 4, Robin = 6, Beth = 10, Carmen = 5, José = 5 Total = 4 + 6 + 10 + 5 + 5 = 30 If Bob = 3, Robin = 5, Beth = 8, Carmen = 4, José = 4 Total = 3 + 5 + 8 + 4 + 4 = 24
Use words, pictures, or numbers to explain your answer.	Write an equation: Bob = B; Robin = $B + 2$; Beth = $(B + 2) + B$; José + Carmen = $(B + 2) + B$ $B + B + 2 + B + 2 + B + B + 2 + B = 24$ $6B + 6 = 24$ $6B = 18$; $B = 3$
Does your answer make sense? Why or why not?	Yes—you can check by adding all the sales: Bob = 3; Robin = 5; Beth = 8; Carmen = 4; José = 4. Total = 24.
Answer the Problem	☑ Be sure to give your answer on the previous page

Algebra
Extended-Response Practice Problem 40

40. Danisha wants to join a CD club, but she is not sure whether she will save money by joining. The cost of joining the club is a one-time fee of $24.95, and CDs cost $11.00 each. The local music store has a CD sale twice a year. All CDs are only $14.95 each. The CDs at the store are regularly priced at $18.95. How many CDs does Danisha need to buy from the club before she saves money? Would you join the club if you were Danisha? Explain your reasons.

Use the thinking map on the next page to solve the problem.
Write your answer in the box.

Thinking Map

Read the Problem	☐ Read the Problem
Reread the Problem	☐ Reread the Problem
Write the important math vocabulary that tells you what to do.	
Reread the Problem	☐ Reread the Problem
What information do you have that you can use to solve the problem? Can you get clues from: ☐ The answer choices ☐ Pictures, charts, or graphs ☐ A problem you have solved before	
Reread the Problem	☐ Reread the Problem
Solve the problem. Use one or more: ☐ Act it out. ☐ Use manipulatives. You can: ☐ Do a calculation: addition, subtraction, multiplication, or division. ☐ Draw a picture, graph, or table. ☐ Set up an equation. ☐ Write a formula.	
Use words, pictures, or numbers to explain your answer.	
Does your answer make sense? Why or why not?	
Answer the Problem	☐ Be sure to give your answer on the previous page

Chapter 5

Data and Probability

What is Data and Probability?

- You will analyze data and make predictions about the likelihood of possible outcomes (probability) using ratios and fractional parts.

- You will use various data collection techniques, use a variety of tables or graphs to record the information collected, and be able to interpret the recorded data.

- You will use some statistical methods to describe your data sets (e.g., mean, median, mode).

What does Data and Probability look like?

- You ask questions that require data collection.

- You read, interpret, and compare the data from various sources.

- You collect data from classroom surveys, observations, and/or measurements.

- You organize the data you collected.

- You develop your own frequency tables, charts, and circle or line graphs to display your data.

- You conduct simple probability experiments and predict possible outcomes.

Model Problem 13:
Data and Probability
Multiple-Choice

13. Which fraction below gives the greatest probability of a desired outcome?

○ A. $\frac{3}{9}$

○ B. $\frac{3}{12}$

○ C. $\frac{4}{16}$

○ D. $\frac{5}{20}$

Use the thinking map on the next page to solve the problem.
Fill in the circle next to the correct answer.
Mark only one answer.

DO NOT COPY

Thinking Map

Read the Problem	☐ Read the Problem
Reread the Problem	☐ Reread the Problem
Write the important math vocabulary that tells you what to do.	
Reread the Problem	☐ Reread the Problem
What information do you have that you can use to solve the problem? Can you get clues from: ☐ The answer choices ☐ Pictures, charts, or graphs ☐ A problem you have solved before	
Reread the Problem	☐ Reread the Problem
Solve the problem. Use one or more: ☐ Act it out. ☐ Use manipulatives. You can: ☐ Do a calculation: addition, subtraction, multiplication, or division. ☐ Draw a picture, graph, or table. ☐ Set up an equation. ☐ Write a formula.	
Use words, pictures, or numbers to explain your answer.	
Does your answer make sense? Why or why not?	
Answer the Problem	☐ Be sure to give your answer on the previous page

One Way to Complete the Thinking Map

Read the Problem	☑ Read the Problem
Reread the Problem	☑ Reread the Problem
Write the important math vocabulary that tells you what to do.	fraction greatest probability desired outcome
Reread the Problem	☑ Reread the Problem
What information do you have that you can use to solve the problem? Can you get clues from: ☐ The answer choices ☑ Pictures, charts, or graphs ☑ A problem you have solved before	$\dfrac{3}{9}$, $\dfrac{3}{12}$, $\dfrac{4}{16}$, $\dfrac{5}{20}$
Reread the Problem	☑ Reread the Problem
Solve the problem. Use one or more: ☐ Act it out. ☐ Use manipulatives. You can: ☐ Do a calculation: addition, subtraction, multiplication, or division. ☐ Draw a picture, graph, or table. ☐ Set up an equation. ☐ Write a formula.	To solve the problem, compare fractions. To compare fractions, change to percentages or reduce them. Fractions: Percents: $\dfrac{3}{9}=\dfrac{1}{3}$ $\dfrac{4}{16}=\dfrac{1}{4}$ $\dfrac{3}{9}=33.33\%$ $\dfrac{3}{12}=\dfrac{1}{4}$ $\dfrac{5}{20}=\dfrac{1}{4}$ $\dfrac{3}{12},\ \dfrac{4}{16},\ \dfrac{5}{20}=25\%$
Use words, pictures, or numbers to explain your answer.	$\dfrac{1}{3}$, or 33.33%, is larger than $\dfrac{1}{4}$, or 25%. $\dfrac{3}{12}$, $\dfrac{4}{16}$, and $\dfrac{5}{20}=25\%$
Does your answer make sense? Why or why not?	Yes—fractions can be compared more easily when they are reduced or when they are changed to percents.
Answer the Problem	☑ Be sure to give your answer on the previous page

Data and Probability
Multiple-Choice Practice Problem 41

41. There are three coins in Bobbie's purse: a penny, a nickel, and a dime. What is the probability that she will get 25 cents if she grabs any one of the coins out of her purse?

○ A. $\dfrac{1}{3}$

○ B. $\dfrac{1}{1}$

○ C. $\dfrac{0}{3}$

○ D. $\dfrac{3}{3}$

Use the thinking map on the next page to solve the problem.
Fill in the circle next to the correct answer.
Mark only one answer.

Thinking Map

Read the Problem	☐ Read the Problem
Reread the Problem	☐ Reread the Problem
Write the important math vocabulary that tells you what to do.	
Reread the Problem	☐ Reread the Problem
What information do you have that you can use to solve the problem? Can you get clues from: ☐ The answer choices ☐ Pictures, charts, or graphs ☐ A problem you have solved before	
Reread the Problem	☐ Reread the Problem
Solve the problem. Use one or more: ☐ Act it out. ☐ Use manipulatives. You can: ☐ Do a calculation: addition, subtraction, multiplication, or division. ☐ Draw a picture, graph, or table. ☐ Set up an equation. ☐ Write a formula.	
Use words, pictures, or numbers to explain your answer.	
Does your answer make sense? Why or why not?	
Answer the Problem	☐ Be sure to give your answer on the previous page

Data and Probability
Multiple-Choice Practice Problem 42

42. There are four black pens in the teacher's desk drawer. What is the probability that Peggy will get a black pen if she takes a pen out of the drawer without looking?

○ A. $\dfrac{1}{4}$

○ B. $\dfrac{1}{5}$

○ C. $\dfrac{1}{1}$

○ D. $\dfrac{0}{0}$

Use the thinking map on the next page to solve the problem.
Fill in the circle next to the correct answer.
Mark only one answer.

Thinking Map

Read the Problem	☐ Read the Problem
Reread the Problem	☐ Reread the Problem
Write the important math vocabulary that tells you what to do.	
Reread the Problem	☐ Reread the Problem
What information do you have that you can use to solve the problem? Can you get clues from: ☐ The answer choices ☐ Pictures, charts, or graphs ☐ A problem you have solved before	
Reread the Problem	☐ Reread the Problem
Solve the problem. Use one or more: ☐ Act it out. ☐ Use manipulatives. **You can:** ☐ Do a calculation: addition, subtraction, multiplication, or division. ☐ Draw a picture, graph, or table. ☐ Set up an equation. ☐ Write a formula.	
Use words, pictures, or numbers to explain your answer.	
Does your answer make sense? Why or why not?	
Answer the Problem	☐ Be sure to give your answer on the previous page

Data and Probability
Multiple-Choice Practice Problem 43

43. At a school fundraiser, 220 tickets were sold for a drawing. You bought 5 tickets. What are your chances of winning?

- ○ A. 5%

- ○ B. 50%

- ○ C. 2%

- ○ D. 20%

Use the thinking map on the next page to solve the problem.
Fill in the circle next to the correct answer.
Mark only one answer.

DO NOT COPY

Thinking Map

Read the Problem	☐ Read the Problem
Reread the Problem	☐ Reread the Problem
Write the important math vocabulary that tells you what to do.	
Reread the Problem	☐ Reread the Problem
What information do you have that you can use to solve the problem? Can you get clues from: ☐ The answer choices ☐ Pictures, charts, or graphs ☐ A problem you have solved before	
Reread the Problem	☐ Reread the Problem
Solve the problem. Use one or more: ☐ Act it out. ☐ Use manipulatives. You can: ☐ Do a calculation: addition, subtraction, multiplication, or division. ☐ Draw a picture, graph, or table. ☐ Set up an equation. ☐ Write a formula.	
Use words, pictures, or numbers to explain your answer.	
Does your answer make sense? Why or why not?	
Answer the Problem	☐ Be sure to give your answer on the previous page

 © 2005 Englefield & Associates, Inc.

Data and Probability
Multiple-Choice Practice Problem 44

44. Select the graph that shows change in the weight of a child over a five-year period.

○ A.

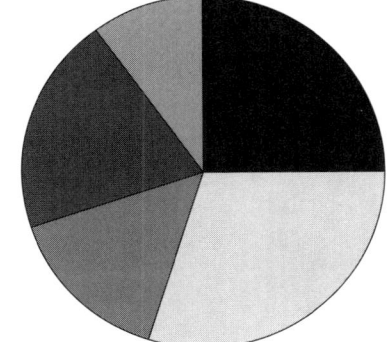

○ B.

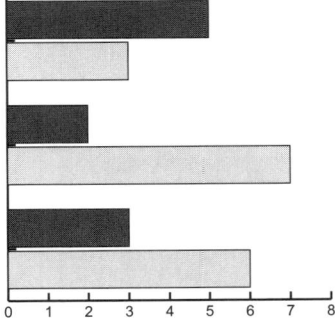

○ C.

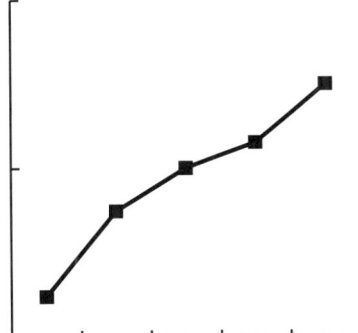

○ D.

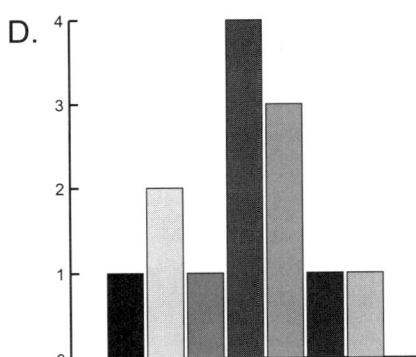

**Use the thinking map on the next page to solve the problem.
Fill in the circle next to the correct answer.
Mark only one answer.**

Thinking Map

Read the Problem	☐ Read the Problem
Reread the Problem	☐ Reread the Problem
Write the important math vocabulary that tells you what to do.	
Reread the Problem	☐ Reread the Problem
What information do you have that you can use to solve the problem? Can you get clues from: ☐ The answer choices ☐ Pictures, charts, or graphs ☐ A problem you have solved before	
Reread the Problem	☐ Reread the Problem
Solve the problem. Use one or more: ☐ Act it out. ☐ Use manipulatives. You can: ☐ Do a calculation: addition, subtraction, multiplication, or division. ☐ Draw a picture, graph, or table. ☐ Set up an equation. ☐ Write a formula.	
Use words, pictures, or numbers to explain your answer.	
Does your answer make sense? Why or why not?	
Answer the Problem	☐ Be sure to give your answer on the previous page

Data and Probability
Multiple-Choice Practice Problem 45

45. If you spin each spinner once, what is your probability of landing on Blue and D?

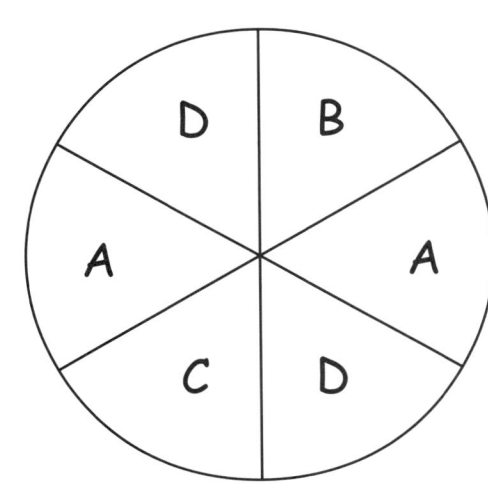

○ A. $\frac{1}{12}$

○ B. $\frac{1}{6}$

○ C. $\frac{4}{10}$

○ D. $\frac{1}{4}$

Use the thinking map on the next page to solve the problem.
Fill in the circle next to the correct answer.
Mark only one answer.

Thinking Map

Read the Problem	☐ Read the Problem
Reread the Problem	☐ Reread the Problem
Write the important math vocabulary that tells you what to do.	
Reread the Problem	☐ Reread the Problem
What information do you have that you can use to solve the problem? Can you get clues from: ☐ The answer choices ☐ Pictures, charts, or graphs ☐ A problem you have solved before	
Reread the Problem	☐ Reread the Problem
Solve the problem. Use one or more: ☐ Act it out. ☐ Use manipulatives. You can: ☐ Do a calculation: addition, subtraction, multiplication, or division. ☐ Draw a picture, graph, or table. ☐ Set up an equation. ☐ Write a formula.	
Use words, pictures, or numbers to explain your answer.	
Does your answer make sense? Why or why not?	
Answer the Problem	☐ Be sure to give your answer on the previous page

Data and Probability
Multiple-Choice Practice Problem 46

46. Carly had seven math assignments, with a mean score of 80%. She needed a mean score of 82% to get a B on her report card. Her teacher told her she could complete another assignment to change the mean. What grade does Carly need to get on the new assignment to change her grade to a B?

○ A. 100%

○ B. 82%

○ C. 84%

○ D. 96%

**Use the thinking map on the next page to solve the problem.
Fill in the circle next to the correct answer.
Mark only one answer.**

DO NOT COPY

Thinking Map

Read the Problem	☐ Read the Problem
Reread the Problem	☐ Reread the Problem
Write the important math vocabulary that tells you what to do.	
Reread the Problem	☐ Reread the Problem
What information do you have that you can use to solve the problem? Can you get clues from: ☐ The answer choices ☐ Pictures, charts, or graphs ☐ A problem you have solved before	
Reread the Problem	☐ Reread the Problem
Solve the problem. Use one or more: ☐ Act it out. ☐ Use manipulatives. **You can:** ☐ Do a calculation: addition, subtraction, multiplication, or division. ☐ Draw a picture, graph, or table. ☐ Set up an equation. ☐ Write a formula.	
Use words, pictures, or numbers to explain your answer.	
Does your answer make sense? Why or why not?	
Answer the Problem	☐ Be sure to give your answer on the previous page

Data and Probability
Multiple-Choice Practice Problem 47

47. Twelve students wanted to carry the flag for the Labor Day parade. The teacher put a series of numbers in a box and said that the student who chose the median number could carry the flag. The numbers are shown below. Who drew the median number?

18, 16, 13, 12, 11, 11, 9, 8, 7, 7, 7, 6

○ A. the first child who drew a 7

○ B. the child who drew a 9

○ C. the child who drew a 9.5

○ D. No one picked the median number.

Use the thinking map on the next page to solve the problem.
Fill in the circle next to the correct answer.
Mark only one answer.

Thinking Map

Read the Problem	☐ Read the Problem
Reread the Problem	☐ Reread the Problem
Write the important math vocabulary that tells you what to do.	
Reread the Problem	☐ Reread the Problem
What information do you have that you can use to solve the problem? Can you get clues from: ☐ The answer choices ☐ Pictures, charts, or graphs ☐ A problem you have solved before	
Reread the Problem	☐ Reread the Problem
Solve the problem. Use one or more: ☐ Act it out. ☐ Use manipulatives. You can: ☐ Do a calculation: addition, subtraction, multiplication, or division. ☐ Draw a picture, graph, or table. ☐ Set up an equation. ☐ Write a formula.	
Use words, pictures, or numbers to explain your answer.	
Does your answer make sense? Why or why not?	
Answer the Problem	☐ Be sure to give your answer on the previous page

Model Problem 14:
Data and Probability
Short-Answer

14. Five students are competing for first and second prize in a hopscotch tournament. How many different combinations of first- and second-place winners are there? What is the probability of being a first-place winner? A second-place winner?

**Use the thinking map on the next page to solve the problem.
Write your answer in the box.**

Thinking Map

Read the Problem	☐ Read the Problem
Reread the Problem	☐ Reread the Problem
Write the important math vocabulary that tells you what to do.	
Reread the Problem	☐ Reread the Problem
What information do you have that you can use to solve the problem? Can you get clues from: ☐ The answer choices ☐ Pictures, charts, or graphs ☐ A problem you have solved before	
Reread the Problem	☐ Reread the Problem
Solve the problem. Use one or more: ☐ Act it out. ☐ Use manipulatives. You can: ☐ Do a calculation: addition, subtraction, multiplication, or division. ☐ Draw a picture, graph, or table. ☐ Set up an equation. ☐ Write a formula.	
Use words, pictures, or numbers to explain your answer.	
Does your answer make sense? Why or why not?	
Answer the Problem	☐ Be sure to give your answer on the previous page

One Way to Complete the Thinking Map

Read the Problem	☑ Read the Problem
Reread the Problem	☑ Reread the Problem
Write the important math vocabulary that tells you what to do.	how many different combinations first- and second-prize winners
Reread the Problem	☑ Reread the Problem
What information do you have that you can use to solve the problem? Can you get clues from: ☐ The answer choices ☐ Pictures, charts, or graphs ☐ A problem you have solved before	5 students first and second place
Reread the Problem	☑ Reread the Problem
Solve the problem. Use one or more: ☐ Act it out. ☐ Use manipulatives. You can: ☐ Do a calculation: addition, subtraction, multiplication, or division. ☑ Draw a picture, graph, or table. ☐ Set up an equation. ☐ Write a formula.	Label the students A–E. 1st|2nd A: B, C, D, E 1st|2nd B: A, C, D, E 1st|2nd C: A, B, D, E 1st|2nd D: A, B, C, E 1st|2nd E: A, B, C, D
Use words, pictures, or numbers to explain your answer.	There are 20 different combinations of 1st and 2nd place winners. A first place winner has a 4 out of 20 (4/20) chance of being first (4/20 = 1/5). A second place winner has a 4 out of 20 (4/20) chance of being second (4/20 = 1/5).
Does your answer make sense? Why or why not?	Yes—information is based on data, and although it is possible to make a prediction, it is a prediction and not a fact.
Answer the Problem	☑ Be sure to give your answer on the previous page

Data and Probability
Short-Answer Practice Problem 48

48. Chloë played a game with her sister. She had two bags of colored marbles. In one bag, she had two blue marbles and two red marbles. In the other bag, she had two blue marbles and one red marble. If her sister picked one marble from each bag, what are the chances that Chloë could correctly predict that her sister had a pair of blue marbles? Explain your answer.

Use the thinking map on the next page to solve the problem.
Write your answer in the box.

 © 2005 Englefield & Associates, Inc.

Thinking Map

Read the Problem	☐ Read the Problem
Reread the Problem	☐ Reread the Problem
Write the important math vocabulary that tells you what to do.	
Reread the Problem	☐ Reread the Problem
What information do you have that you can use to solve the problem? Can you get clues from: ☐ The answer choices ☐ Pictures, charts, or graphs ☐ A problem you have solved before	
Reread the Problem	☐ Reread the Problem
Solve the problem. Use one or more: ☐ Act it out. ☐ Use manipulatives. You can: ☐ Do a calculation: addition, subtraction, multiplication, or division. ☐ Draw a picture, graph, or table. ☐ Set up an equation. ☐ Write a formula.	
Use words, pictures, or numbers to explain your answer.	
Does your answer make sense? Why or why not?	
Answer the Problem	☐ Be sure to give your answer on the previous page

Data and Probability
Short-Answer Practice Problem 49

49. The lunchroom manager took a survey of the students to determine their favorite cookies. The results are listed below.

   A. Was there a favorite? What was the least favorite?

   B. What can the lunchroom manager infer from the data? What would you serve if you were the lunchroom manager and why?

Favorite Cookies

Chocolate Chip	120 votes
Sugar	35 votes
Oatmeal Raisin	98 votes
Peanut Butter	110 votes
Ginger Snaps	28 votes

**Use the thinking map on the next page to solve the problem.
Write your answer in the box.**

DO NOT COPY

Thinking Map

Read the Problem	☐ Read the Problem
Reread the Problem	☐ Reread the Problem
Write the important math vocabulary that tells you what to do.	
Reread the Problem	☐ Reread the Problem
What information do you have that you can use to solve the problem? Can you get clues from: ☐ The answer choices ☐ Pictures, charts, or graphs ☐ A problem you have solved before	
Reread the Problem	☐ Reread the Problem
Solve the problem. Use one or more: ☐ Act it out. ☐ Use manipulatives. You can: ☐ Do a calculation: addition, subtraction, multiplication, or division. ☐ Draw a picture, graph, or table. ☐ Set up an equation. ☐ Write a formula.	
Use words, pictures, or numbers to explain your answer.	
Does your answer make sense? Why or why not?	
Answer the Problem	☐ Be sure to give your answer on the previous page

Model Problem 15: Data and Probability Extended-Response

15. Larry's boss pays him a commission of 5% on his average sales (mean) every week. His sales figures for last week are shown in the chart.

   Larry told his friend, "I had such a bad day Wednesday; I should have stayed home." How would Larry's commission be affected if he had stayed home Wednesday? (If he had stayed home, his sales would be $00.00 for the day.) Would Larry's pay per day be greater if he hadn't worked on Wednesday? Would Larry have earned more this week if he hadn't worked on Wednesday?

Monday	$1500
Tuesday	$3000
Wednesday	$800
Thursday	$2500
Friday	$1500

Use the thinking map on the next page to solve the problem. Write your answer in the box.

Thinking Map

Read the Problem	☐ Read the Problem
Reread the Problem	☐ Reread the Problem
Write the important math vocabulary that tells you what to do.	
Reread the Problem	☐ Reread the Problem
What information do you have that you can use to solve the problem? Can you get clues from: ☐ The answer choices ☐ Pictures, charts, or graphs ☐ A problem you have solved before	
Reread the Problem	☐ Reread the Problem
Solve the problem. Use one or more: ☐ Act it out. ☐ Use manipulatives. You can: ☐ Do a calculation: addition, subtraction, multiplication, or division. ☐ Draw a picture, graph, or table. ☐ Set up an equation. ☐ Write a formula.	
Use words, pictures, or numbers to explain your answer.	
Does your answer make sense? Why or why not?	
Answer the Problem	☐ Be sure to give your answer on the previous page

One Way to Complete the Thinking Map

Read the Problem	☑ Read the Problem
Reread the Problem	☑ Reread the Problem
Write the important math vocabulary that tells you what to do.	commission of 5% average sales
Reread the Problem	☑ Reread the Problem
What information do you have that you can use to solve the problem? Can you get clues from: ☐ The answer choices ☑ Pictures, charts, or graphs ☑ A problem you have solved before	Monday Tuesday Wednesday } weekly sales Thursday Friday Zero sales on Wednesday if he stays home.
Reread the Problem	☑ Reread the Problem
Solve the problem. Use one or more: ☐ Act it out. ☐ Use manipulatives. You can: ☐ Do a calculation: addition, subtraction, multiplication, or division. ☐ Draw a picture, graph, or table. ☐ Set up an equation. ☐ Write a formula.	average = $(1500 + 3000 + 800 + 2500 + 1500) \div 5$ average = $9300 \div 5 = \$1,860$ Without Wednesday: average = $(1500 + 3000 + 0 + 2500 + 1500) \div 5$ average = $\$1,700$
Use words, pictures, or numbers to explain your answer.	5 day week = $\$9,300 \div 5 = \$1,860$ per day 4 day week = $\$8,500 \div 4 = \$2,125$ per day commission for 5 day week = $\$1,860 \times .05 = \$93$ commission for 4 day week = $\$1,700 \times .05 = \$85$ He makes more per week and more commission by working 5 days. He makes more per day by working 4 days.
Does your answer make sense? Why or why not?	Yes, because a low score, especially a zero, has a great effect on the mean score (and on his commission).
Answer the Problem	☑ Be sure to give your answer on the previous page

Data and Probability
Extended-Response Practice Problem 50

50. The fifth-grade students played chess during indoor recess all winter. The graph shows how many games each student won out of a total of 20 games. The students decided to have a tournament in the spring. Use the data from the graph to predict the following information.

1. Based on the data, is it equally likely that Noah and Delaney could win the tournament? Explain.

2. Between Joey and Tonya, who would you predict to win? Explain.

3. Is it possible for Missy to win? Is it likely? Explain the difference.

4. Based on the data, who would you predict will win the tournament? Explain your answer.

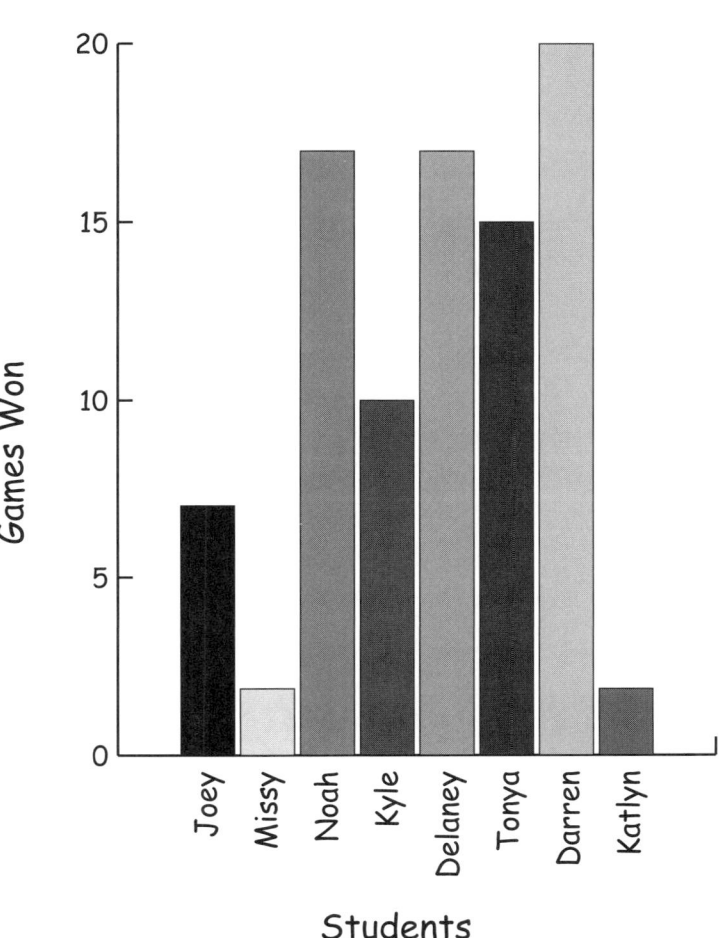

Use the thinking map on page 151 to solve the problem.
Write your answer in the box on the next page.

Data and Probability
Extended-Response Practice Problem 50

50. (continued)

Use the thinking map on the next page to solve the problem.
Fill in the circle next to the correct answer.
Mark only one answer.

DO NOT COPY © 2005 Englefield & Associates, Inc.

Thinking Map

Read the Problem	☐ Read the Problem
Reread the Problem	☐ Reread the Problem
Write the important math vocabulary that tells you what to do.	
Reread the Problem	☐ Reread the Problem
What information do you have that you can use to solve the problem? Can you get clues from: ☐ The answer choices ☐ Pictures, charts, or graphs ☐ A problem you have solved before	
Reread the Problem	☐ Reread the Problem
Solve the problem. Use one or more: ☐ Act it out. ☐ Use manipulatives. You can: ☐ Do a calculation: addition, subtraction, multiplication, or division. ☐ Draw a picture, graph, or table. ☐ Set up an equation. ☐ Write a formula.	
Use words, pictures, or numbers to explain your answer.	
Does your answer make sense? Why or why not?	
Answer the Problem	☐ Be sure to give your answer on the previous page

Chapter 6

Manipulatives

In this section, you will find tools that you can use to help you solve the problems in the book. Remember that you can use tools like this in your mind or on paper at other times when you need to solve mathematical problems. The manipulatives that you will find in this section are described below. Follow your teacher's directions on how and when to use these tools.

Two-Dimensional Figures

You can use the two-dimensional figures on page 155 as a reference when a problem mentions a square, a rhombus, or any other shape that is included. You can cut out the shapes, or you can just see what each figure looks like as you solve any mathematics problem that mentions that shape.

One-Inch and Half-Inch Grid Paper

You can use the one-inch and half-inch grids on pages 157 and 159 to make 3-dimensional shapes or to draw areas for problems that require you to figure out size. Your teacher will direct you on how to use these grids in different types of problems.

Spinners

Four kinds of spinners are included on page 163 so that you can see what happens when you spin with different probabilities. For example, in Figure 2 (shown below and also on page 163), the likelihood of landing on the number 3 is 2 out of 4, or 1/2.

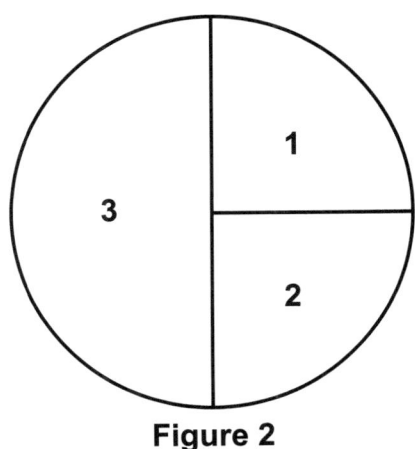

Figure 2

Figures 1, 3, and 4 (page 163) demonstrate equal chances of landing on any of the numbers or colors. These spinners can also be used for you to play games or experiment with probability as you record the number of times the spinner lands on each of the numbers or colors (if you choose to color them in).

Measurement Tools

The protractor on page 161 is included so you can measure various angles. The inch and centimeter rulers (also on page 161) are included so you can use them as a reference for solving problems that involve measurements.

Volume of Cubes

The cube models on page 165 are included so you can see how volume changes in different shapes.

Clock (Face with Hands)

The clock model on page 167 is included so you can make a clock to use when you work out the time problems that are included in your book.

2-Dimensional Figures

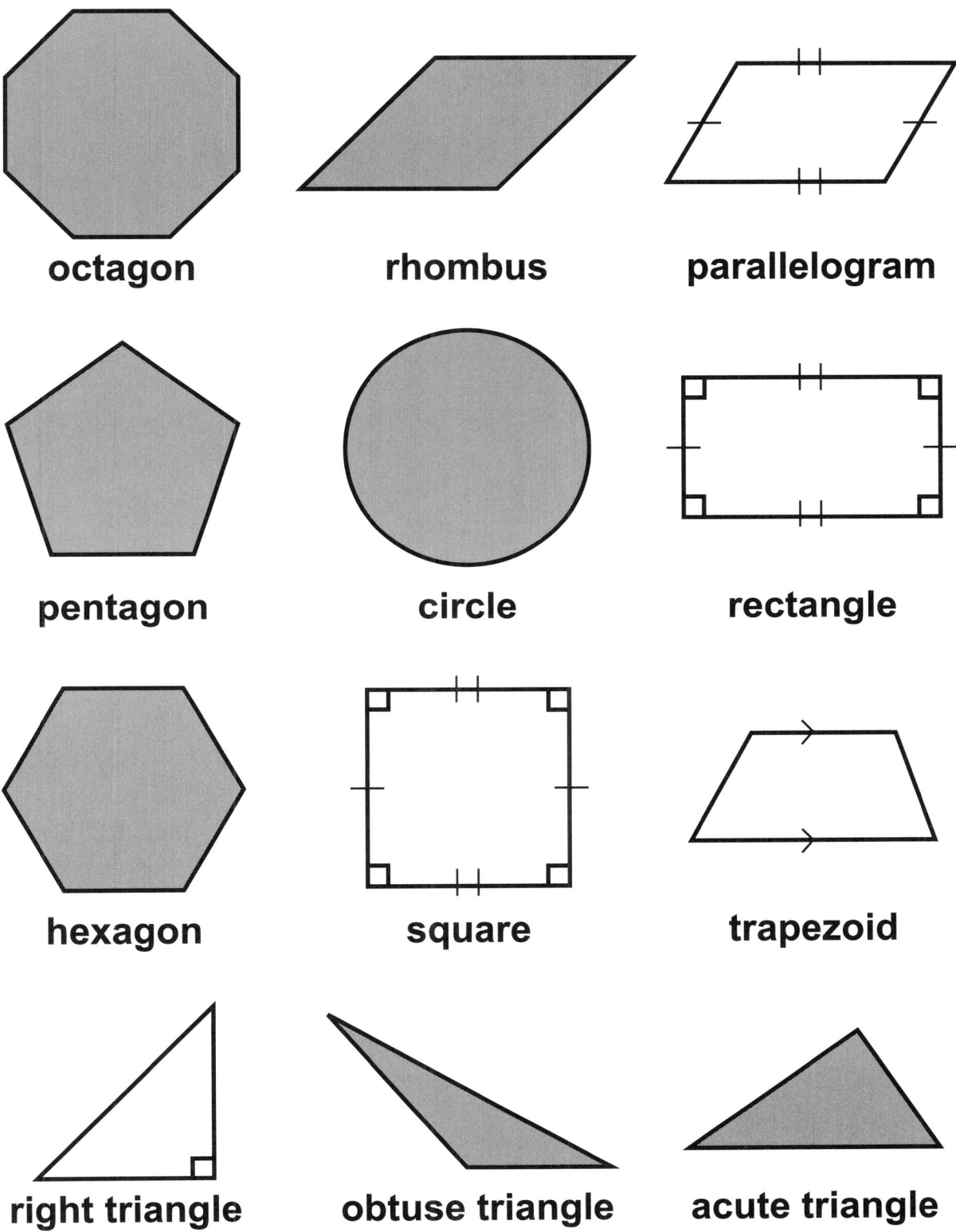

octagon

rhombus

parallelogram

pentagon

circle

rectangle

hexagon

square

trapezoid

right triangle

obtuse triangle

acute triangle

One-Inch Grid

Half-Inch Grid

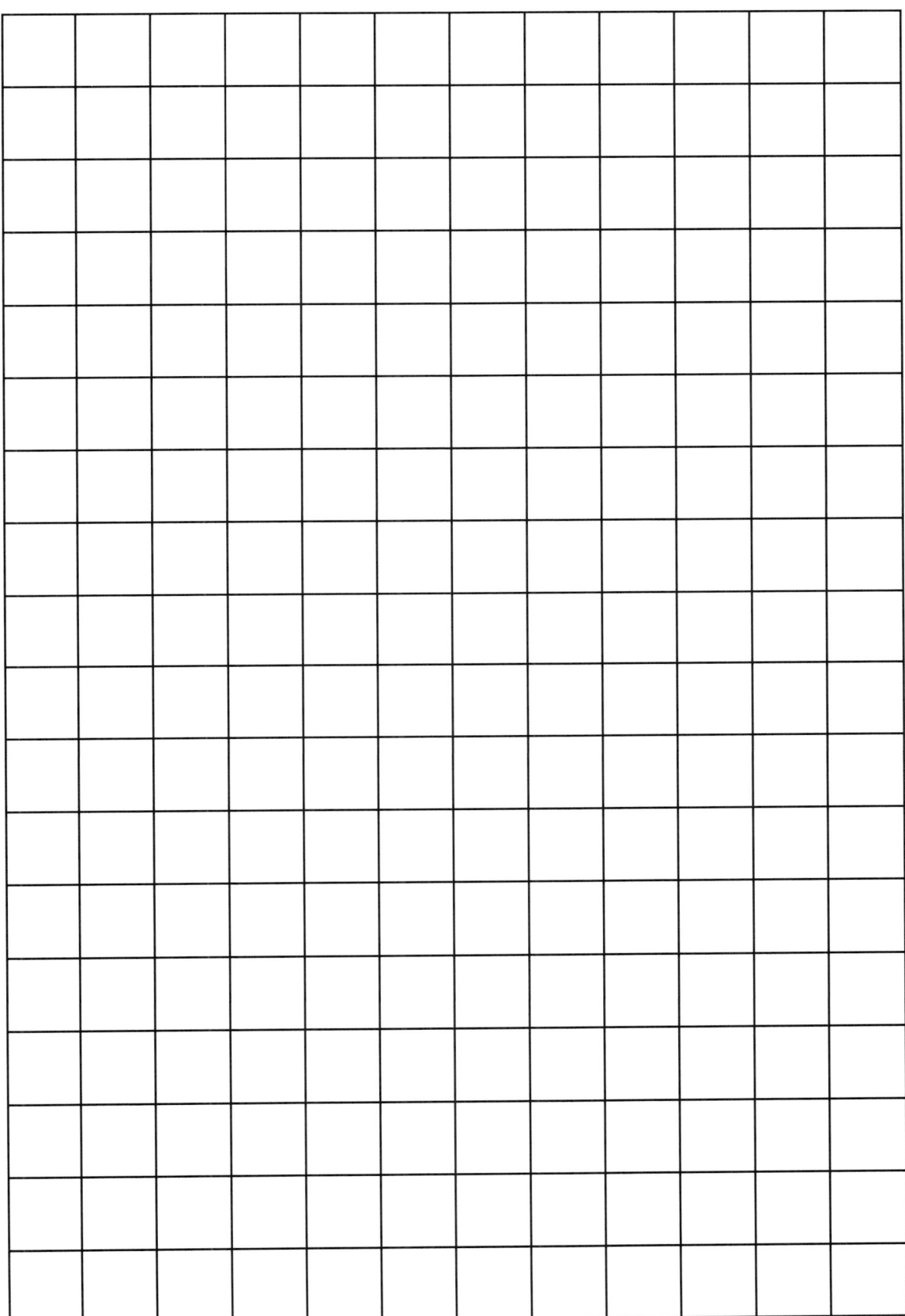

Measurement Tools

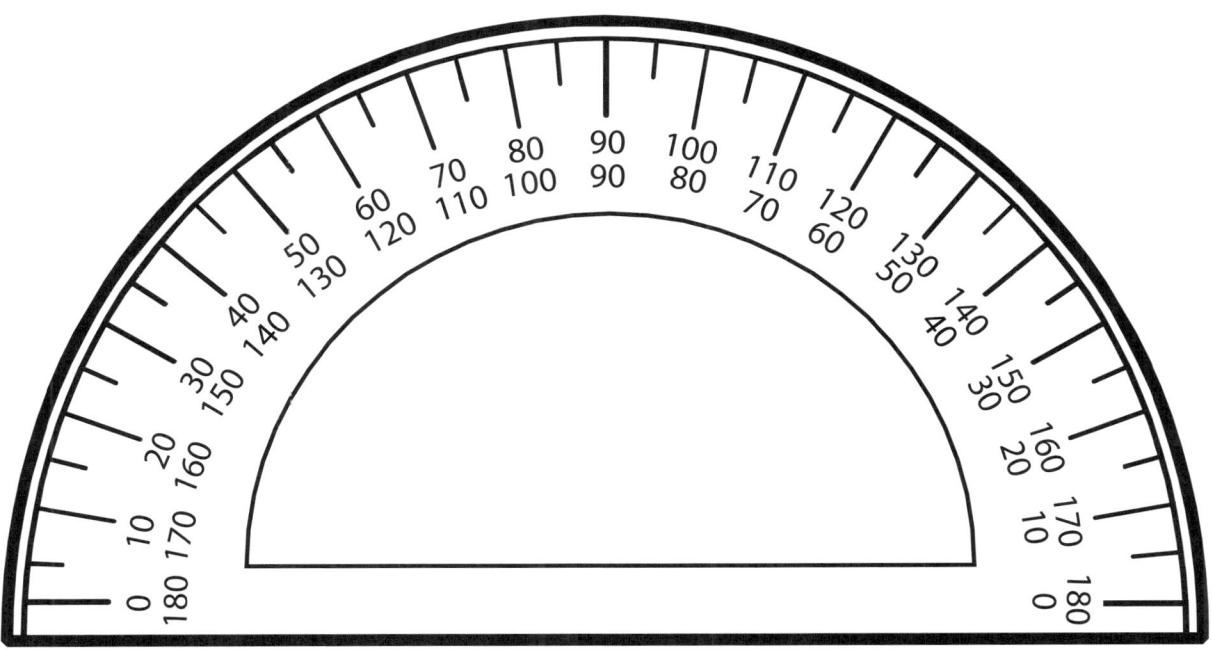

Protractor

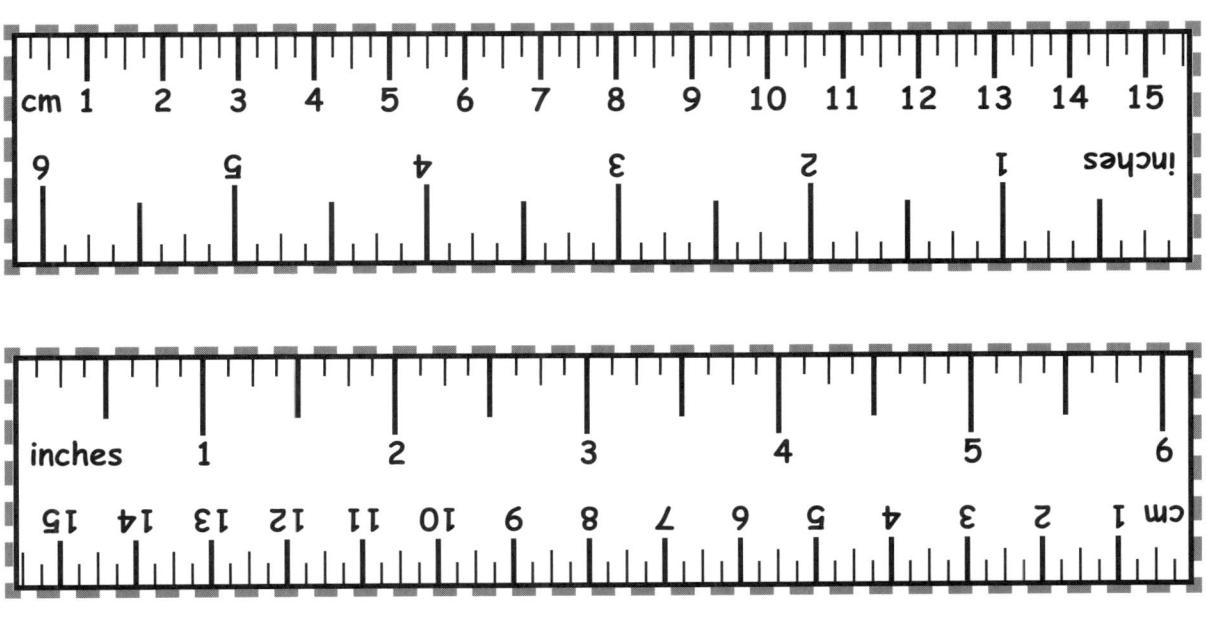

Inch/Centimeter Rulers

Spinners for Probability

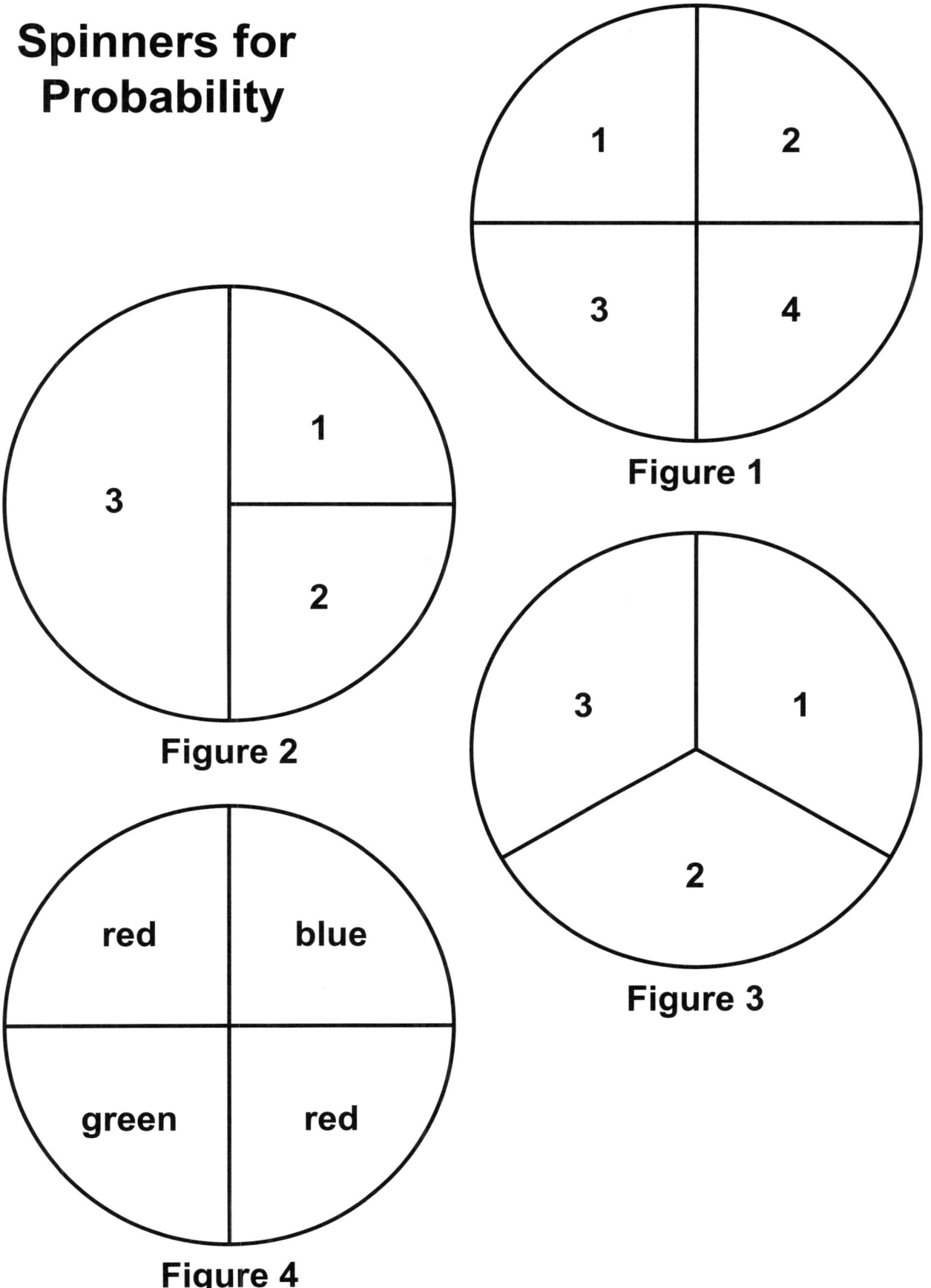

Figure 1

Figure 2

Figure 3

Figure 4

Volume of Cubes

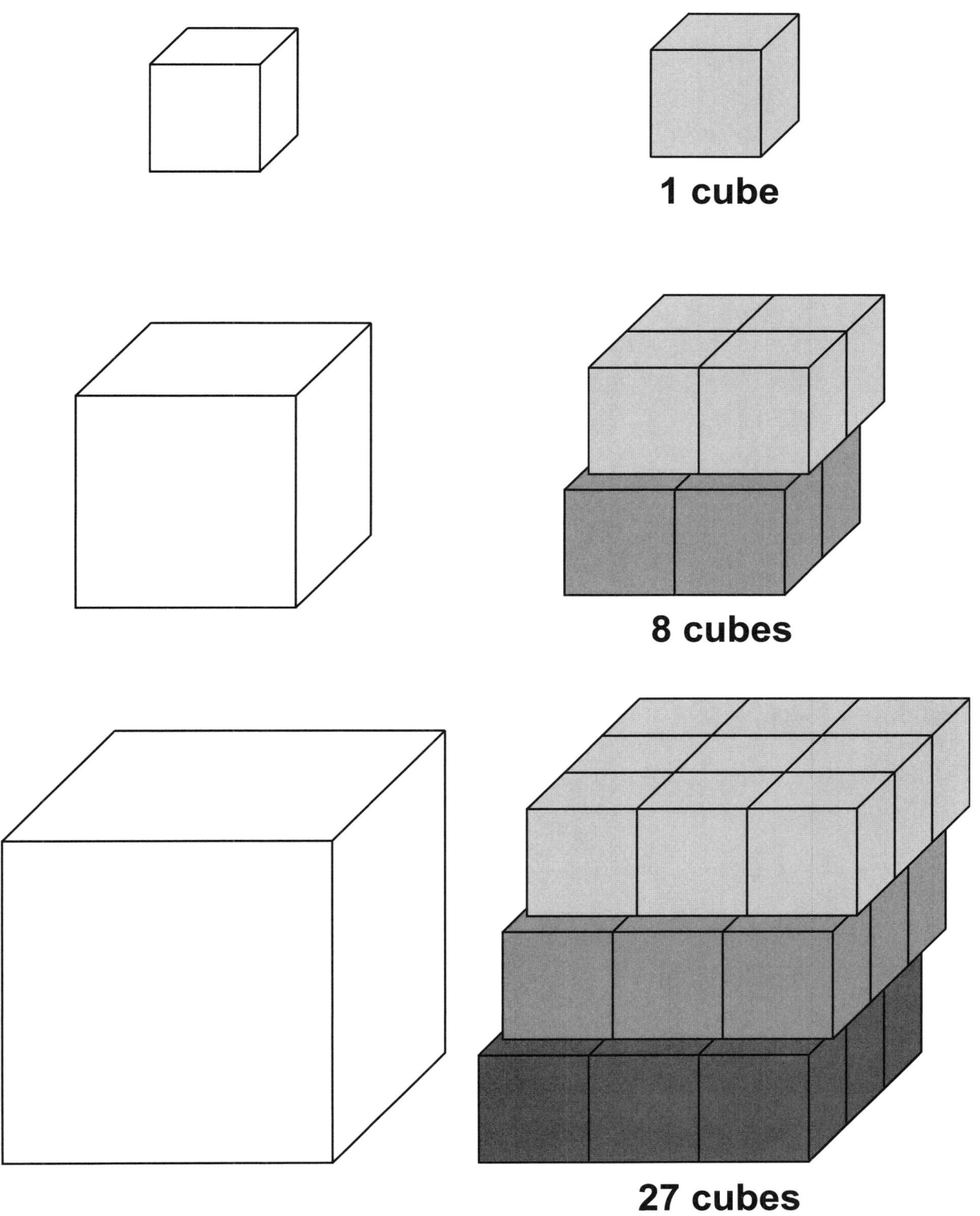

1 cube

8 cubes

27 cubes

Clock

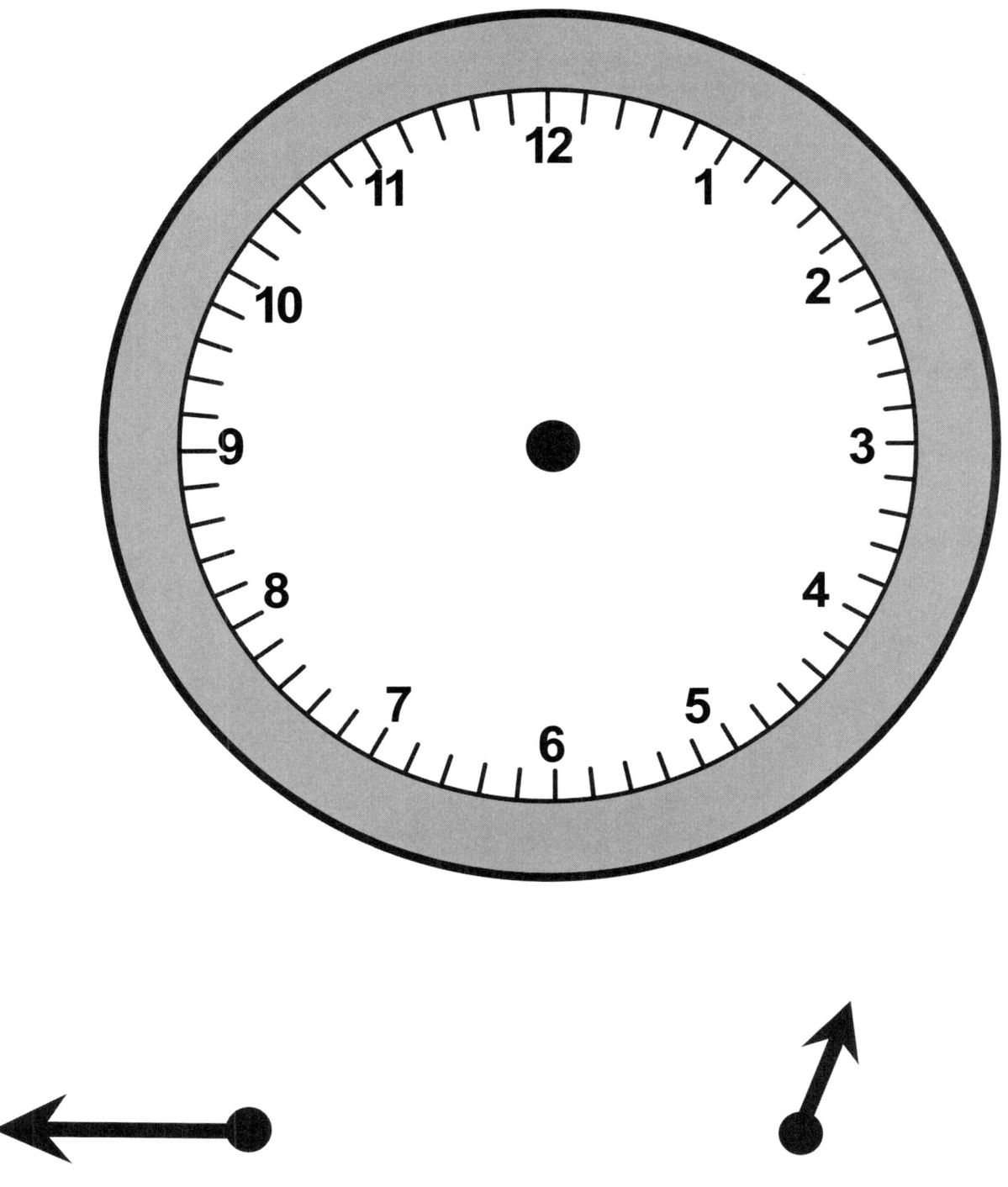

Thank YOU
For Your Purchase!

For more information on our products,

call 1-877-PASSING (727-7464), or

visit our website:

www.showwhatyouknowpublishing.com